DO NO WRONG

ETHICS FOR PROSECUTORS AND DEFENDERS

PETER A. JOY AND KEVIN C McMUNIGAL

ABA
AMERICAN BAR ASSOCIATION
Criminal Justice Section

Cover design by ABA Publishing.

The materials contained herein represent the opinions and views of the authors and/or the editors, and should not be construed to be the views or opinions of the law firms or companies with whom such persons are in partnership with, associated with, or employed by, nor of the American Bar Association or the Criminal Justice Section, unless adopted pursuant to the bylaws of the Association.

Printed in the United States of America

Library of Congress Cataloging-in-Publication Data

Joy, Peter A.
Do No Wrong: Ethics for Prosecutors and Defenders / Peter A. Joy and Kevin C. McMunigal. — 1st ed.
p. cm.
Includes index.
ISBN 978-1-60442-269-6
1. Criminal procedure—United States. 2. Legal ethics—United States. 3. Public prosecutors—Professional ethics—United States. 4. Defense (Criminal procedure)—United States. I. McMunigal, Kevin C., 1950– II. Title.

KF9619.J69 2008
345.73'05—dc22

2008050811

Discounts are available for books ordered in bulk. Special consideration is given to state bars, CLE programs, and other bar-related organizations. Inquire at Book Publishing, ABA Publishing, American Bar Association, 321 North Clark Street, Chicago, Illinois 60654-7598.

www.ababooks.org

CONTENTS

ACKNOWLEDGMENTS

In 2001, Paul Giannelli, serving on the Editorial Board for the American Bar Association publication *Criminal Justice*, asked us to consider writing an ethics column for the quarterly magazine. We agreed, the Editorial Board accepted our first submission, and the ethics column has been a regular feature ever since.

We have been fortunate to have MaryAnn Dadisman edit our columns from the start, and thank her for her thoughtful, careful work. Although the columns have been reworked and updated for this book, her contributions along the way laid the groundwork for this book.

We deeply appreciate the support of our law schools, Case Western Reserve University and Washington University in St. Louis, and our deans over the years—at Case Western, Jerry Korngold and Gary Simpson; at Washington University, Dan Keating, Joel Seligman, and Kent Syverud. In addition, Peter Joy offers special thanks to Chris Peper and the Christian B. Peper Academic Support Endowment for supporting his work on this book. Kevin McMunigal offers special thanks to Roe Green, whose generosity in Judge Ben C. Green's honor has helped support Kevin's work on this book.

We thank the Criminal Justice Section Book Publications Committee for supporting this publication, and Art Garwin, Director of the ABA Center for Professional Responsibility, for reviewing each chapter and making a number of helpful suggestions. We also thank the editor of this book, Sarah Forbes Orwig, as well as Tim Brandhorst, Associate Director of ABA Book Publishing, for their support of this project. Kevin McMunigal wishes to thank Mary Lombardi for her research work on many of these chapters.

Finally, we thank the judges, defense counsel, prosecutors, and law professors who serve as leaders of the American Bar Association Criminal Justice Section and as members of the Criminal Justice Section's various committees. These lawyers share the goal of improving our criminal justice system. We are pleased to be associated with their efforts and hope that the publication of this book contributes toward that goal.

Peter A. Joy
St. Louis, Missouri
August 2008

Kevin C. McMunigal
Cleveland, Ohio
August 2008

ABOUT THE AUTHORS

Professor Peter A. Joy is Professor of Law and Director of the Criminal Justice Clinic at Washington University School of Law in St. Louis, Missouri, where he teaches Legal Profession, Comparative Legal Ethics Seminar, Trial Practice & Procedure, and supervises clinical students representing clients in misdemeanor and felony cases. Prior to teaching, Mr. Joy litigated both criminal and civil cases in private practice. For several years, he directed the clinical program at Case Western Reserve University. He is a Contributing Editor of the ABA's *Criminal Justice* magazine, serves on the *Clinical Law Review* Board of Editors, and has been a Program Director for the National Institute of Trial Advocacy (NITA). Mr. Joy writes primarily about criminal justice, legal ethics, and legal education issues. He has an A.B. from Youngstown State University and a J.D. from Case Western Reserve University.

Kevin C. McMunigal is the Judge Ben C. Green Professor of Law at Case Western Reserve University School of Law in Cleveland, Ohio, where he teaches Criminal Law, Evidence, and Professional Responsibility. Before entering teaching, Mr. McMunigal was an Assistant U.S. Attorney for several years in California. Earlier, he clerked for a federal district judge and was in private practice. He is a Contributing Editor of the ABA's *Criminal Justice* magazine and is the coauthor of a criminal law casebook, *Criminal Law: A Contemporary Approach, Cases, Statutes & Problems*, published by Aspen. He writes primarily in the areas of legal ethics, criminal law, and evidence. Mr. McMunigal has a B.A. from Stanford University and a J.D. from Boalt Hall School of Law at the University of California, Berkeley.

INTRODUCTION

Criminal law practice is a minefield of legal ethics issues for both the prosecution and defense. How far may the prosecution or defense go in using religion in closing argument? Does the defense lawyer or the client decide whether to raise an insanity defense or to present mitigation evidence? Is the defendant entitled to *Brady* material prior to entering a plea bargain? When may the defense introduce evidence of an alternate perpetrator or SODDI (the "some other dude did it") defense? Answering these and other similar ethical questions requires not only an understanding of the relevant ethics rules but also applicable constitutional and statutory law as well as rules of criminal procedure and evidence.

This book aims to put these and other ethical questions on the "radar screens" of criminal practioners and to provide both prosecution and defense with the analysis and authorities necessary to understand the issues and underlying policies. This book gathers in one place ethics columns we wrote over a number of years for the ABA Criminal Justice Section's publication *Criminal Justice*. Each has been updated and some expanded. A list of research resources appears at the end of each chapter. In addition to exploring ethical issues that prosecutors and defense attorneys routinely face, we also examine emerging areas of ethics, suchas lawyer involvement in client media campaigns, and ongoing policy debates over the proper roles for prosecution and defense counsel.

Throughout the book, we refer to the ABA Model Rules of Professional Conduct, which almost every U.S. jurisdiction has adopted in some form. Because there is variation among states in the language of some of the rules, the reader is advised to check the specific language of the relevant ethical rule in the lawyer's jurisdiction as well as case law and the jurisdiction's ethics opinions. In many instances, the ABA Standards for Criminal Justice provide useful guidance, and we have cited to the relevant provisions of those standards when they are helpful to understanding an issue.

PART 1

Prosecution's Role

CHAPTER 1

Are a Prosecutor's Responsibilities "Special"?

Are the responsibilities of prosecutors special? If so, how? Standards for the ethical conduct of prosecutors are often described as different from the standards for criminal defense lawyers and civil advocates. Reference is often made to the "special responsibilities" and "extraordinary duties" of prosecutors, and both courts and ethical rules admonish a prosecutor to be a "minister of justice" and to "seek justice." Such descriptions and rhetoric, though, overstate the differences between the responsibilities of prosecutors and those of other lawyers, and they fail to convey that in many, perhaps most, instances the standard of conduct for prosecutors is identical to that for civil advocates and criminal defense lawyers. Generalizations about a prosecutor's special ethical duties also mask the fact that when prosecutorial standards do differ from those governing other lawyers, it is typically in degree rather than in kind.

In this chapter, we offer a view of the rules governing prosecutors that is more nuanced than traditional views describing prosecutorial ethics as simply different, special, or extraordinary. We do not address here the various rationales that might be offered for creating distinct rules for prosecutors—a topic we turn to in the next chapter.

Few Ethics Rules Specifically Address Prosecutors

It is helpful at the outset to note that specific and detailed rules directly addressing the obligations of prosecutors do not exist for most areas of prosecutorial conduct. Model Rule 3.8, entitled

"Special Responsibilities of a Prosecutor," addresses only eight topics and fails to address many questions prosecutors routinely face, such as conduct during plea negotiations and the boundaries of closing argument at trial. In addition to the scarcity of specific rules, it can be difficult to locate all of the legal and ethical standards addressing particular areas of prosecutorial conduct because they are scattered among a wide variety of sources, including constitutional case law, statutes, ethics, criminal procedure, and evidence rules, as well as internal prosecutorial guidelines. The disclosure obligations of a federal prosecutor, for example, are controlled by the *Brady v. Maryland*, 373 U.S. 83 (1963), line of constitutional cases, the Jencks Act, Federal Rules of Criminal Procedure 16 and 26.2, Federal Rule of Evidence 404(b), the *United States Attorneys' Manual*, as well as applicable ethical rules.

Even when one finds a specific provision, it may fail to give prosecutors adequate notice or guidance concerning their ethical obligations. Cases and ethics opinions dealing with prosecutorial conduct often resolve issues by simply noting that a particular course of action is dictated by the prosecutor's special obligation to seek justice or the prosecutor's special role as a minister of justice, without explaining the reasoning that connects relatively abstract ideas of justice to an appropriate course of conduct in a particular situation.

Enforcement of prosecutorial standards has also been lax, raising additional problems for assessing the current state of prosecutorial ethics. Model Rule 3.8(d), for example, sets forth an obligation to disclose exculpatory evidence or information that appears to be broader than the constitutional *Brady* disclosure obligation. But enforcement of this obligation through professional discipline of prosecutors is scant. There are few ethics opinions or cases addressing its contours. Cases addressing disclosure of exculpatory information often focus exclusively on the constitutional dimension and ignore the separate ethical duty. It is hard to resolve ambiguities concerning disclosure obligations with no body of ethics opinions or case law to provide guidance. For example, whether Model Rule 3.8(d) requires disclosure of exculpatory information prior to entry of a guilty plea remains unaddressed, although this rule and a similar predecessor provision in the 1969 Model Code have been in effect for almost 40 years and prosecutors resolve hundreds of thousands of cases through use of guilty pleas every day.

These problems create areas of ambiguity regarding prosecutorial standards. Nonetheless, some things are clear.

Prosecutors Often Subject to Same Rules as Other Lawyers

More often than not, prosecutor standards do not differ from those applicable to other lawyers. Ethics codes such as the 1969 Model Code of Professional Responsibility and the Model Rules of Professional Conduct, most recently updated in February 2008, contain a few special rules for prosecutors along with a wide range of rules applicable to all lawyers. Prosecutors are subject to both these special rules and these general rules. Some rules of general applicability, such as those on advertising and fees, are not of concern to prosecutors because they neither advertise nor collect fees from clients. But many rules of general applicability are of concern to prosecutors because they deal with work that prosecutors routinely do—work that is often indistinguishable from the work other lawyers do.

Words such as *special* and *extraordinary* used in describing the rules and duties applicable to prosecutors suggest that those rules and duties are peculiar, unique, uncommon—completely distinct from the rules and duties applicable to criminal defense counsel and civil advocates. But simply browsing the table of contents of the ABA Model Rules reveals that the provisions unique to prosecutors are relatively few—confined to eight provisions set forth in Model Rule 3.8. It also reveals that there are many rules that apply equally to all lawyers. Examples include the ethics rules on competence, diligence, and candor toward a tribunal as well as the advocate witness rule.

Berger v. United States

Berger v. United States, 295 U.S. 78 (1935), is the most frequently cited authority in cases, ethics opinions, and academic writing for the special obligations of prosecutors. It has been described as "the locus classicus for discussion of the extraordinary duties of a prosecutor." (CHARLES W. WOLFRAM, MODERN LEGAL ETHICS, § 13.10 at 760 (1986).) Oddly enough, though, the case is an example of a prosecutor being held to account under a rule of general applicability rather than a rule that applies specifically to prosecutors.

The *Berger* case, best known for the quote that although a prosecutor "may strike hard blows, he is not at liberty to strike foul ones," enforced an obligation that is quite ordinary and applies equally to all advocates—the obligation of lawyers in a trial not to assert their personal knowledge of facts in issue. The prosecutor did a number of improper things warranting criticism, but Justice Sutherland, writing for the majority, focused primarily on the prosecutor's assertion in closing argument of his personal knowledge of a fact he had attempted but failed to prove during the trial's evidentiary phase.

The prosecutor had called a witness named Goldstein to identify the defendant, but, according to Justice Sutherland, Goldstein "had difficulty in doing so." Nonetheless, the prosecutor was apparently convinced that Goldstein knew the defendant and told the jury as much in his closing argument, stating, "[Y]ou can bet your bottom dollar she knew Berger" and describing the witness as "a woman that I knew, knew Berger and could identify him."

Justice Sutherland reasoned based on these statements that "the jury was . . . invited to conclude that the witness Goldstein knew Berger well, but pretended otherwise; and that this was within the personal knowledge of the prosecuting attorney." Both the Model Rules and the Model Code prohibit prosecutors from asserting personal knowledge of facts at issue during a trial. But that duty is imposed not only on prosecutors, as later references to *Berger* seem to suggest. The relevant Model Rules provision is not found in Rule 3.8 covering the "Special Responsibilities of a Prosecutor," but in Rule 3.4, captioned "Fairness to Opposing Party and Counsel," which sets rules applicable to all lawyers. The critical prosecutorial ethical obligation in *Berger* was the same as that imposed on criminal defense lawyers and civil advocates.

Extraordinary Remedies

If not offered to justify the imposition of some extraordinary duty on the prosecutor, what, then, was the purpose of Justice Sutherland's classic description of the prosecutor? The court of appeals had concluded that the prosecutor engaged in misconduct but nonetheless affirmed Berger's conviction because it thought it unlikely that the prosecutor's misconduct had affected the outcome of Berger's trial. The Supreme Court disagreed and ordered a new trial based on a much higher assessment of the probability that the misconduct affected the outcome in the case. Sutherland used the classic passage in *Berger* to introduce his discussion of the appropriate remedy and to justify his departure from the court of appeals on that issue.

Because of the status of the prosecutor as a government representative, Justice Sutherland thought the jury much more likely to accept the prosecutor's improper assertions than if he had been a private lawyer representing a criminal defendant or a private party. Because of his special status, the prosecutor's "improper suggestions, insinuations and, especially, assertions of personal knowledge are apt to carry much weight against the accused when they should properly carry none." Justice Sutherland found "prejudice to the cause of the accused ... so highly probable that we are not justified in assuming its non-existence." Rather than defining an extraordinary obligation, *Berger* is a case about imposing an extraordinary remedy for breach of an ordinary obligation.

Model Rule 3.8

Model Rule 3.8 does contain provisions applicable only to prosecutors because certain tasks are unique to the prosecutor's office. Model Rule 3.8(e), for example, restricts a prosecutor's use of a grand jury subpoena to compel a lawyer "to present evidence about a past or present client" unless certain conditions are fulfilled. This restriction applies only to prosecutors because only prosecutors have access to grand jury subpoena power. Model Rule 3.8(c) states that a prosecutor shall "not seek to obtain from an unrepresented accused a waiver of important pretrial rights, such as the right to a preliminary hearing." Here, again, this restriction is unique to prosecutors because the only lawyer who is in a position to obtain such a waiver from "an unrepresented accused" is a prosecutor.

In 2008, the ABA adopted two new and related responsibilities for prosecutors. Model Rule 3.8(g) requires a prosecutor who comes to know of "new, credible and material evidence creating a reasonable likelihood that a convicted defendant did not commit an offense" to "promptly disclose that evidence to an appropriate authority, and ... if the conviction was obtained in the prosecutor's jurisdiction, ... promptly disclose that evidence to the defendant unless a court authorizes delay, and ... undertake further investigation, or make reasonable efforts to cause an investigation, to determine whether the defendant was convicted of an offense that the defendant did not commit." Model Rule 3.8(h) requires a prosecutor "to seek to remedy the conviction" when "a prosecutor knows of clear and convincing evidence establishing that a defendant in the prosecutor's jurisdiction was convicted of an offense the defendant did not commit." These provisions recognize that as a representative of the government, the prosecutor has a unique obligation to take remedial measures when there has been a miscarriage of justice.

Despite the title of Model Rule 3.8, "Special Responsibilities of a Prosecutor," other provisions that appear in Model Rule 3.8 are not truly peculiar or unique to prosecutors. For example, Model Rule 3.8(a) states that the prosecutor must "refrain from prosecuting a charge that the prosecutor knows is not supported by probable cause." Here the prosecutor is required to act as a "gatekeeper" and ensure that a charge has adequate legal and factual support. At first glance, this provision appears similar to Model Rule 3.8(c) and (e), discussed above, because the only lawyer who can prosecute a criminal case is a prosecutor.

Model Rule 3.1 applies similar gatekeeping duties to all lawyers, requiring them to have "a basis in law and fact . . . that is not frivolous" before advancing a claim or argument on behalf of a client. And Rule 11 of the Federal Rules of Civil Procedure creates a duty for civil advocates to screen their filings to make sure they are "well grounded in fact and . . . warranted by existing law or a good faith argument for the extension, modification, or reversal of existing law." The probable cause standard applied to prosecutors may be more demanding than the standards used under Model Rule 3.1 and Rule 11, but still the prosecutor's gatekeeping duty is not unique. The difference, if any, is one of degree rather than kind.

Model Rule 3.8(f) is another provision that creates a duty not peculiar or unique to prosecutors. Model Rule 3.8(f) restricts public comments by prosecutors "that have a substantial likelihood of heightening public condemnation of the accused." It also creates a duty to exercise reasonable care to prevent police and others associated with the prosecutor from making statements that would violate either Rule 3.8(f) or Model Rule 3.6, the general provision on public comment applicable to all lawyers.

Again, at first glance, this rule seems unique to prosecutors because it talks about comments concerning an "accused" and exercising control over public comment by police. A criminal defense lawyer or a civil advocate is not, for example, in a position to exercise control over the police regarding comments about an accused person. But, again, one finds similar restrictions on both criminal defense lawyers and civil advocates elsewhere in the Model Rules. Model Rule 3.6 sets forth a general bar on a lawyer participating in litigation from making a public statement when doing so creates "a substantial likelihood of materially prejudicing an adjudicative proceeding."

Model Rule 3.6 clearly applies to prosecutors. Comment [5] to Model Rule 3.8 notes that Rule 3.8(f) "supplements Rule 3.6." So in the area of public comment all advocates have the same duty to control their statements about pending cases. Rule 3.6 binds prosecutors, criminal defense counsel, and civil advocates alike. Rule 3.8(f) does impose on the prosecutor an additional burden to avoid heightening public condemnation of an accused, but again the difference here is one of degree rather than kind.

What about the prosecutor's duty under Rule 3.8(f) to control the police? Is that a restriction unique to prosecutors? Model Rules 5.1 and 5.3, which apply to all lawyers, create obligations for lawyers to control other lawyers in their firms as well as nonlawyers "employed or retained by or associated with" the lawyer. Model Rule 8.4(a) makes it professional misconduct for a lawyer to violate the ethics rules "through the acts of another." The obligations created by Rules 5.1, 5.3, and 8.4 impose on criminal defense lawyers and civil advocates a duty to take steps to control the public statements of others with whom they work that is quite similar to the prosecutor's duty to control police created by Rule 3.8(f).

When Are a Prosecutor's Duties Distinct?

There are situations in which the prosecutor's obligations are truly distinct, especially when compared with those of a criminal defense lawyer. For example, the prosecutor under *Brady v. Maryland* and Model Rule 3.6(d) is obligated to turn over exculpatory evidence and information. The analog for a defense lawyer would be an obligation to give to the prosecution inculpatory evidence and information. Clearly, the defense lawyer has no such obligation, based on rules of confidentiality and the constitutional prohibition on compelled self-incrimination.

But the prosecutor's duty to turn over exculpatory evidence is not more demanding than what is required of civil litigants under modern federal discovery rules. These require a party, without awaiting a discovery request, to turn over all information and the identity of all witnesses that support or undermine any party's claims or defenses. While the prosecutor's *Brady* disclosure obligation is restricted by a narrow materiality limitation, federal civil discovery rules permit a party to "obtain discovery regarding any matter, not privileged, that is relevant to the claim or defense of any party" even if the information is not admissible at trial "if the discovery appears reasonably calculated to lead to the *discovery* of admissible evidence." (FED. R. CIV. P. 26.)

A stark contrast between prosecutor and criminal defense counsel is found in their respective obligations regarding the filing of a criminal charge and the entry of a "not guilty" plea. If the prosecutor knows that someone is innocent, the prosecutor is obligated not to charge or convict the person. If the prosecutor learns that a charged defendant is innocent, he or she must dismiss the charge. But when a defense lawyer knows that a client is guilty and concludes that the prosecution can prove its case beyond a reasonable doubt, the defense is not barred from entering a not guilty plea, continuing to represent the client, and working toward a dismissal or acquittal. To require anything less of defense counsel would negate the presumption of innocence and the right against self-incrimination, and would relieve the government of the burden of proving guilt beyond a reasonable doubt.

So, are the statements one often encounters about "special responsibilities" and "extraordinary duties" of prosecutors simply empty rhetoric? Such statements often are misleading overgeneralizations, but our view is that they express a poorly articulated but widely shared view on the part of judges, lawyers, and the public. In areas in which prosecutors exercise discretion and their conduct is not covered by general ethics rules or the special rules for prosecutors found in ethics codes, we expect the prosecutor to act as a monitor both of substantive and procedural justice in ways not expected of either criminal defense lawyers or civil advocates. Though seldom described in detail, it is this monitoring obligation that creates for the prosecutor a responsibility that properly is characterized as different, special, and extraordinary in comparison with other litigating lawyers.

Conclusion

The notion that there is something exceptional about a prosecutor's ethical obligations is critical in understanding those obligations, but overgeneralization and overstatement can mask the fact that in many situations the prosecutor is subject to precisely the same rules as other litigating lawyers. We address the rationales for creating distinct obligation for prosecutors in the next chapter.

Resources for Chapter 1

Rules and Standards

Model Rules of Professional Conduct 3.1, 3.4, 3.6, 3.8, 5.1, 5.3, and 8.4(a).

Federal Rules of Civil Procedure 11 and 26.

Federal Rules of Criminal Procedure 16 and 26.2.

Federal Rule of Evidence 404(b).

Cases and Ethics Opinions

Berger v. United States, 295 U.S. 78 (1935).
Brady v. Maryland, 373 U.S. 83 (1963).

Articles, Reports, Books, and Other Sources

Bennett L. Gershman, *The Prosecutor's Duty to the Truth*, 14 Geo. J. Legal Ethics 309 (2001).

Kevin C. McMunigal, *Are Prosecutorial Standards Different?*, 68 Fordham L. Rev. 1453 (2000).

Charles W. Wolfram, Modern Legal Ethics, § 13.10 at 760 (1986).

The Jencks Act, 18 U.S.C. Section 3500.

CHAPTER 2

Why Should Prosecutors "Seek Justice"?

We often exhort a prosecutor to be a "minister of justice" and to "seek justice." What do these admonitions mean? In the previous chapter, we discussed whether and how prosecutors' standards of ethical conduct differ from those governing civil litigators and criminal defense lawyers. We noted that few ethics rules specifically address prosecutors, that in most situations prosecutors are subject to precisely the same rules as other litigating lawyers, and that the differences between prosecutors' obligations and the obligations of criminal defense lawyers and civil advocates often occur when prosecutors exercise discretion. In this chapter, we address the rationales for creating distinct obligations for prosecutors.

Under the adversary system, lawyers are expected to pursue their client's interests without concern for the fairness or accuracy of the result. A prosecutor is expected at times to step out of this conventional adversarial role and to act as a monitor both of substantive and procedural justice in ways not expected of criminal defense lawyers or civil advocates.

Compare, for example, the ethical obligations of a prosecutor with those of a civil litigator or a criminal defense lawyer when engaged in cross-examination. All lawyers, no matter the client they represent, are required by Model Rule 4.4 not to "use means that have no substantial purpose other than to embarrass, delay, or burden a third person." This rule applies equally to all lawyers, including prosecutors. But the ABA Criminal Justice Standards distinguish between a prosecutor and a defense lawyer when cross-examining a truthful witness. The ethical standards for the cross-examination of witnesses under the ABA Criminal

Justice Standards for the Defense Function, Standard 4-7.6(b), and Standards for the Prosecution Function, Standard 3-5.7(b), state that a defense lawyer's "belief or knowledge" or a prosecutor's "belief that the witness is telling the truth does not preclude cross-examination." The Defense Function Standard stops here and provides no further limit on a defense lawyer's cross-examination of a truthful witness. In contrast, the Prosecution Function Standard 3-5.7(b) continues that a prosecutor's belief that the witness is telling the truth "may affect the method and scope of cross-examination" and a "prosecutor should not use the power of cross-examination to discredit or undermine a witness if the prosecutor knows the witness is testifying truthfully."

In short, a prosecutor is prohibited from discrediting through cross-examination a witness believed to be telling the truth, whereas a criminal defense lawyer is not. The Criminal Justice Standards on cross-examination of a truthful witness compel the prosecutor to step outside an adversarial role of pursuing a conviction and, instead, require a prosecutor to act in a way that helps maintain the integrity of the adversarial truth-finding process.

A prosecutor's disclosure obligations are also distinct from those of a criminal defense lawyer. *Brady v. Maryland,* 373 U.S. 83 (1963), and Model Rule 3.8(d) require a prosecutor to turn over exculpatory evidence and information, whereas there is no corresponding obligation for a defense lawyer to give the prosecution inculpatory evidence and information.

What rationales drive these distinct rules for prosecutors?

Rationales for Treating Prosecutors Differently

The Government's Overarching Interest in Justice

A primary rationale for requiring a prosecutor at times to act differently than a defense lawyer flows from the fact that a prosecutor represents the government and not an individual client. All lawyers must under Model Rule 1.2 allow the client to determine the objectives of the representation. Usually, a client charged with a crime directs the lawyer to seek acquittal on any charges and to minimize punishment if convicted, regardless of the client's guilt or the punishment the client may deserve. When the client is the government, determining the client's interests is not so simple. In representing the government, a prosecutor represents all of the citizenry—including, in a sense, the accused. In this role of representing the citizenry, a prosecutor must decide what is in the public's interest and then advance that position. In making these decisions, courts and ethics rules direct a prosecutor to act fairly and impartially, and to seek procedural as well as substantive justice for the accused. For example, in *Berger v. United States*, 295 U.S. 78, 88 (1935), the Supreme Court stated that the government's interest "in a criminal prosecution is not that it shall win a case, but that justice shall be done." *Berger* and other court decisions reflect the belief that the citizenry, and therefore the government, has an overarching interest in justice.

Ethics rules also assume that a prosecutor's special interest in justice does not end with simply convicting those legally responsible. Comment [1] to Model Rule 3.8 states that the prosecutor is not simply "an advocate" but also a "minister of justice" who has "specific obligations to see that the defendant is accorded procedural justice and that guilt is decided upon the basis of sufficient evidence."

Protecting Against Abuse of Power

Another major rationale for requiring a prosecutor to act differently than a defense lawyer flows from the significant power accorded to a prosecutor. A prosecutor is usually the most powerful player in the criminal justice system, deciding whom to prosecute, what crimes to charge, and greatly influencing sentencing of those found guilty. In using these powers, a prosecutor must exercise discretion. Special obligations to seek justice by acting evenhandedly are necessary to check against potential abuse of power, especially discretionary power. The obligations to seek both procedural and substantive justice for the accused serve as guideposts in exercising power. As Comment [1] to Model Rule 3.8 states, a prosecutor has the responsibility as a "minister of justice" to protect the rights of the accused even while seeking to convict the accused. One might argue that this instructs a prosecutor to look beyond merely winning or losing a case, something not required of a defense lawyer.

Asymmetry of Resources

A third rationale for requiring a prosecutor to have different ethical obligations than a defense lawyer derives from the imbalance in resources between the government and the accused one typically finds in criminal cases. The adversarial system tends to assume a rough symmetry in resources, so that each side can muster the competing evidence and arguments the judge and jury need to hear in order to do justice in the case. But the reality in many criminal cases is that criminal defendants and their lawyers lack the resources to investigate cases adequately and present relevant evidence and arguments. Placing special disclosure obligations on prosecutors and requiring them to step out of the adversarial role can be justified by a desire to help prevent asymmetry in resources from distorting the working of the adversary system.

Public Confidence in the Justice System

A fourth rationale for requiring a prosecutor to have different ethical obligations than a defense lawyer can be based on the need to reinforce public confidence in the justice system. Confidence in the justice system and public respect for the law are important in any justice system that relies in large part, as ours does, on voluntary compliance of the citizenry. Public confidence will arguably be increased if the justice system is seen as both fair and accurate. Requiring prosecutors to provide a sort of safety net against procedural unfairness and inaccuracy may increase public confidence in the criminal justice system as a whole. This respect could be eroded if prosecutors were seen as lawyers interested in winning even at the expense of the truth. The public might also react quite negatively to prosecutors acting in a highly adversarial way, indifferent to the fairness and accuracy of criminal convictions and punishment, such as cross-examining a truthful witness or concealing exculpatory information from the accused.

Promotes Open Government

A fifth rationale for requiring a prosecutor to behave differently than a defense lawyer flows from the openness and transparency often associated with a democratic government. The Freedom of Information Act, open meeting laws, and the right to public trial are examples of the public's right to know information bearing on government decisions and actions of government officials. Prosecutors are public officials, typically elected officials, and it may be argued that the public has a right to information in possession of the prosecutor in order to evaluate fully the prosecutor's actions. This right of access to information is particularly important when one is accused of a crime. This is one reason why *Brady v. Maryland*, as well as ethics and discovery rules, require the prosecution to disclose information to the accused. Such disclosure in turn increases the chance that the information will become publicly known at a trial or sentencing hearing.

Although important to the accused, *Brady* and other disclosure obligations give force to the public's interest in obtaining information in possession of the government. In recent years, the revelation of erroneous convictions through use of DNA evidence illustrates the importance of the public's right to information. The public, as well as the accused, has an interest in information and evidence that would prevent an erroneous conviction. At the trial level, the public is represented by the jury, which may gain access to exculpatory evidence in the hands of the prosecution only if the prosecution has an obligation to disclose it to the accused. Thus, a prosecutor's higher disclosure duty promotes both open government and the public's interests in fairness to the accused.

Risks of Injustice

As we have outlined, there are a number of rationales for treating a prosecutor differently than a defense lawyer. More is at risk when a prosecutor, as opposed to a defense lawyer, refuses to step out of the adversarial role. When a defense lawyer refuses to step out of the adversarial role, for example, by cross-examining the truthful witness, the risk is typically that a guilty person will go free. When a prosecutor refuses to step out of the adversarial role, in comparison, again by cross-examining the truthful witness, the risk may be that an innocent person will be convicted. Our system of justice does not weigh these two risks equally. The justice system is more concerned with avoiding conviction of the innocent than it is with assuring conviction of the guilty. Our comparative valuation of these risks may drive us to require the prosecutor to act differently than a defense lawyer.

Given the number of rationales for expecting more of a prosecutor than of other lawyers, one may wonder why the ethics rules do not require more of prosecutors than they currently do. There are very few truly special ethical obligations for prosecutors, and they are rarely enforced by bar discipline processes. For example, studies demonstrate that prosecutors are rarely disciplined for *Brady* violations. Reversal of a conviction, rather than discipline, is the usual remedy for prosecutorial overreaching.

Conclusion

There are a number of rationales in favor of creating distinct ethical obligations for prosecutors. In the previous chapter, we demonstrated that descriptions of a prosecutor as a "minister of justice" who is to "seek justice" tend to overstate the differences between the standard of conduct for prosecutors and other lawyers. In most instances, the standard of conduct for prosecutors is identical to the standard of conduct for civil advocates and defense lawyers. When prosecutorial standards do differ, they do so typically in degree rather in kind from those of other litigating lawyers. Yet, there are some distinct differences, such the limits on cross-examination of a truthful witness and greater disclosure obligations required by *Brady* and ethics rules. When there are differences, a prosecutor is required not to undermine the truth, to accord procedural justice to the accused, and to guard against convicting the innocent.

Resources for Chapter 2

Rules and Standards

MODEL RULES OF PROFESSIONAL CONDUCT 1.2, 3.8(d), and 4.4.

ABA CRIMINAL JUSTICE STANDARDS FOR THE DEFENSE FUNCTION, Standard 4-7.6(b).

ABA CRIMINAL JUSTICE STANDARDS FOR THE PROSECUTION FUNCTION, Standard 3-5.7(b).

Cases and Ethics Opinions

Berger v. United States, 295 U.S. 78 (1935).

Brady v. Maryland, 373 U.S. 83 (1963).

Articles, Reports, Books, and Other Sources

Richard A. Rosen, *Disciplinary Sanctions Against Prosecutors for* Brady *Violations: A Paper Tiger*, 65 N.D. L. REV. 693 (1987).

Bruce A. Green, *Why Should Prosecutors Seek Justice?*, 26 FORDHAM URB. L.J. 607 (1999).

Fred C. Zacharias, *Structuring the Ethics of Prosecutorial Trial Practice: Can Prosecutors Do Justice?*, 44 VAND. L. REV. 45 (1991).

CHAPTER 3

New Rules for Scientific and Exculpatory Evidence?

DNA evidence in recent years has revealed a shocking number of wrongful criminal convictions from across the country. Every few weeks, it seems, the national news reports another erroneous conviction. Examination of these wrongful conviction cases in turn has revealed an array of factors that led the criminal justice process astray. The now familiar litany includes jailhouse informants, coerced confessions, eyewitness identification errors, and inadequate representation.

Prosecutorial misconduct in dealing with both scientific and exculpatory evidence has also played a role in bringing about wrongful convictions. Many prosecutors undoubtedly act ethically regarding scientific and exculpatory evidence and, in doing so, help maintain the integrity of our criminal justice system. But a disturbingly large number of cases reveal prosecutors who fail to adhere to these obligations. In this chapter we address two proposals for changing current ethics rules on how prosecutors should handle scientific and exculpatory evidence.

Scientific Evidence

One proposal by Professors Paul Giannelli and Kevin McMunigal of Case Western Reserve University School of Law is to create a new ethics rule governing the use of false scientific evidence by prosecutors. (*See* Paul C. Giannelli & Kevin C. McMunigal, *Prosecutors, Ethics, and Expert Witnesses*, 76 FORDHAM L. REV., 1493 (2007).) The recommendation would require a gatekeeping role for prosecutors when offering scientific evidence.

The suggested mechanism for implementing such a role would be to modify Model Rule of Professional Conduct 3.8, which governs the special responsibilities of the prosecutor, to include the following new section:

> A prosecutor shall not offer scientific evidence unless he or she has a good faith and reasonable belief that the evidence (1) is based upon sufficient facts or data, (2) is the product of reliable principles and methods, and (3) is the product of reliable application of such principles and methods to the facts of the case.

In sum, the proposal would add a provision to the Model Rules that would make it an ethics violation for a prosecutor to knowingly, recklessly, or negligently offer defective scientific evidence. As the wording of the rule amendment suggests, the gatekeeping role envisioned for prosecutors would be analogous to the one created for trial judges by Federal Rule of Evidence 702, regulating expert testimony.

This proposed rule would significantly alter the prosecutor's obligations regarding false scientific evidence. Model Rule 3.3(a)(3) currently controls prosecutorial use of scientific evidence. Rule 3.3(a)(3) provides the following:

> (a) A lawyer shall not knowingly: . . .
>
> (3) offer evidence that the lawyer *knows* to be false. If a lawyer, the lawyer's client, or a witness called by the lawyer, has offered material evidence and the lawyer comes to *know* of its falsity, the lawyer shall take reasonable remedial measures, including, if necessary, disclosure to the tribunal. A lawyer may refuse to offer evidence, other than the testimony of a defendant in a criminal matter, that the lawyer reasonably believes is false. (Emphasis added.)

Model Rule 3.3(a)(3) applies the same standard to prosecutors as it does to civil litigators and criminal defense lawyers. Although Model Rule 3.8 sets forth the distinct obligations of prosecutors, it does not currently address presentation of false evidence, thereby leaving Model Rule 3.3(a)(3) as the only ethics rule governing prosecutors' use of evidence.

As its text makes clear, Model Rule 3.3(a)(3) places a minimal obligation on prosecutors. If the prosecutor suspects that evidence is false, or even if the prosecutor is aware of a substantial risk that the evidence is false, Model Rule 3.3(a)(3) permits the prosecutor to introduce the evidence. In other words, using Model Penal Code terminology, the prosecutor may introduce evidence if the prosecutor's mental state regarding its falsity is one of innocence, negligence, or even recklessness. Only when the prosecutor's mental state is "knowledge" does Model Rule 3.3(a)(3) bar the prosecutor from offering the evidence. And *knowledge* under Model Rule 1.0 is defined as "actual knowledge of the fact in question."

Why does Model Rule 3.3(a)(3) use such an apparently lax standard regarding false evidence, condoning a lawyer offering evidence when he or she is aware or should be aware of a serious risk that the evidence is false? This aspect of Model Rule 3.3(a)(3) reflects an adversarial paradigm that assigns the task of discovering falsity of evidence primarily to opposing counsel and the fact finder rather than the lawyer offering the evidence. When the prosecutor has knowledge of falsity, he or she must act cooperatively and not introduce false evidence. But when the prosecutor has a mental state less than knowledge, Model Rule 3.3(a)(3) favors an adversarial conception of the lawyer's role by permitting the prosecutor to introduce false evidence.

Instead of allowing the presentation of scientific evidence unless the prosecutor knows it is false, as current Model Rule 3.3(a)(3) does, the Giannelli and McMunigal proposal would bar a prosecutor from offering scientific evidence unless the prosecutor *knows* it is reliable. The proposed rule would effectively create an affirmative obligation on the part of the prosecutor to take reasonable steps to ensure the soundness of the scientific evidence he or she offers.

What arguments support this proposal? First, such a role is appropriate for prosecutors because the quality control mechanisms of the adversary system often do not work in regard to scientific evidence in criminal cases due to lack of defense resources. Criminal defendants and their lawyers routinely lack the resources to cross-examine a prosecution expert effectively, to present competing scientific counterproof, or to point out weaknesses in the prosecution expert's testimony to the fact finder in closing argument. A number of studies have demonstrated this lack of resources and the recurrent failure to provide independent experts to the defense.

Close examination of criminal cases has revealed what is often in effect an ex parte presentation of scientific evidence by the prosecution. The defendant and defense counsel are physically present during the presentation of the evidence, but they cannot participate in anything other than a pro forma fashion due to lack of access to the scientific expertise necessary for cross-examination, presentation of counterproof, and addressing evidentiary weaknesses in closing argument. The lack of an effective challenge by the defense to the prosecution's scientific evidence has the practical impact of nullifying the fact finder's ability to distinguish corrupt from valid scientific evidence.

Investigation sparked largely by DNA evidence has revealed not only that the defense lawyer's and fact finder's ability to monitor the quality of scientific evidence has been seriously compromised, but also that the lack of adversarial challenge has had a corrupting influence on the government's experts. How could an expert such as Fred Zain, a West Virginia State Police forensic expert, for example, repeatedly falsify serology tests in as many as 133 cases if there were effective cross-examination and counterproof from the defense? How would Zain muster the audacity to repeatedly falsify evidence if he was not confident that the supposedly adversarial criminal justice system in which he operated presented no realistic threat that his falsification would be revealed? (In Chapter 5, we discuss how inadequate representation of counsel contributes to wrongful convictions.)

A second rationale for this proposal is that the cooperative role of gatekeeper is consistent with and required by the distinct responsibility all lawyers assume when operating in an ex parte setting. Lawyer ethics rules uniformly recognize a cooperative standard when a lawyer makes an ex parte presentation to a fact finder because the quality control mechanisms of the adversary system are lacking. Model Rule 3.3(d), for example, requires that a lawyer in an ex parte proceeding present all material information to the fact finder, not just what is favorable to the client as the adversary system would dictate. Comment [14] to Model Rule 3.3 states the obvious reasoning behind this cooperative standard: "[T]here is no balance of presentation by opposing advocates." Thus, the lawyer must reveal all facts he or she "reasonably believes are necessary to an informed decision." As pointed out above, although the presentation of scientific evidence takes place in a setting that appears adversarial, in reality it functions in many, perhaps most, cases as an ex parte presentation by the prosecution to the fact finder.

Such an obligation is also consistent with the prosecutor's ethical duty of competence, because a negligent prosecutor is not acting competently. Competence appears as the first of the Model Rules of Professional Conduct, Rule 1.1, and it provides the following: "A lawyer shall provide competent representation to a client. Competent representation requires the legal knowledge, skill, thoroughness and preparation reasonably necessary for the representation." The accompanying Comment [1] explains that relevant factors in determining whether a lawyer acts competently include "the relative complexity and specialized nature of the matter."

Perhaps because the prosecutor's client is the government rather than an individual, we often fail to appreciate that prosecutors who negligently, recklessly, or knowingly use false scientific evidence seriously fail in their ethical obligation to represent the government effectively. Through the conviction of innocent persons, the consequent failure to convict the actual perpetrators, and the creation of cynicism toward the criminal justice system, prosecutors who misuse scientific evidence fail to serve the interests of the governments they represent, as well as the public interest, and thus fail in their ethical obligations.

Exculpatory Evidence

The prosecutorial duty to disclose exculpatory evidence to the defense is well recognized. Model Rule 3.8(d) instructs prosecutors to disclose "all evidence or information known to the prosecutor that tends to negate the guilt of the accused or mitigate the offense." *Brady v. Maryland* and its progeny recognize a parallel constitutional duty to disclose material exculpatory evidence as a requirement of due process. These ethical and constitutional duties are typically seen as requiring disclosure prior to a trial. What happens if a prosecutor discovers exculpatory evidence *after* a defendant has been convicted? Is the prosecutor required to disclose such evidence to a defendant who may be seeking a new trial or to a court reviewing a conviction?

In February 2008, at the ABA Midyear Meeting, the Criminal Justice Section brought a proposed amendment to Model Rule 3.8 to the ABA House of Delegates to deal specifically with this situation. It would require a prosecutor to reveal to the defendant exculpatory evidence learned after the person has been convicted. The amendment, which was adopted by the House, provides the following:

> (g) When a prosecutor knows of new, credible and material evidence creating reasonable likelihood that a convicted defendant did not commit an offense of which the defendant was convicted, the prosecutor shall:
>
> (1) promptly disclose that evidence to an appropriate court or authority, and

(2) if the conviction was obtained in the prosecutor's jurisdiction,
   (i) promptly disclose that evidence to the defendant unless a court authorizes delay, and
   (ii) undertake further investigation, or make reasonable efforts to cause an investigation, to determine whether the defendant was convicted of an offense that the defendant did not commit.

(h) When a prosecutor knows of clear and convincing evidence establishing that a defendant in the prosecutor's jurisdiction was convicted of an offense that the defendant did not commit, the prosecutor shall seek to remedy the conviction.

The report accompanying the changes states, "The obligation to avoid and rectify convictions of innocent people, to which the proposed provisions give expression, is the most fundamental professional obligation of criminal prosecutors." The amendment had support across the full spectrum of the Criminal Justice Section leadership, including prosecutors. The amendment seems particularly appropriate given the large number of erroneous convictions that have been revealed in recent years and the contribution that prosecutorial misconduct regarding exculpatory evidence has made to those erroneous convictions.

Given the roles that prosecutorial misuse of scientific evidence and failure to disclose exculpatory evidence have played in contributing to erroneous criminal convictions, each of the rules discussed in this chapter strikes us as particularly apt additions to Model Rule 3.8's delineation of the ethical obligations of prosecutors.

Resources for Chapter 3

Rules and Standards

Model Rules of Professional Conduct 1.0, 1.1, and 3.3(a)(3).
Federal Rule of Evidence 702.

Cases and Ethics Opinions

Brady v. Maryland, 373 U.S. 83 (1963).

Articles, Reports, Books, and Other Sources

Paul C. Giannelli & Kevin C. McMunigal, *Prosecutors, Ethics, and Expert Witnesses*, 76 Fordham L. Rev. 1493 (2007).

Daniel S. Medwed, *The Zeal Deal: Prosecutorial Resistance to Post-Conviction Claims of Innocence*, 84 B.U.L. REV. 125 (2004).

Fred C. Zacharias, *The Role of Prosecutors in Serving Justice After Convictions*, 58 VAND. L. REV. 171 (2005).

ABA CRIMINAL JUSTICE SECTION'S REPORT TO THE HOUSE OF DELEGATES (February 2008), http://www.abanet.org/crimjust/policy/rule3-8amend.pdf.

PART 2

Defense Counsel's Role

CHAPTER 4

Has *Gideon*'s Promise Been Fulfilled?

More than forty years ago, the Supreme Court decided *Gideon v. Wainwright*, 372 U.S. 335 (1963). Prior to *Gideon*, only defendants facing the death penalty had a right to appointed counsel in state courts. Today, thanks to *Gideon*, public defenders or court-appointed private attorneys represent those unable to afford privately retained lawyers—80 percent of the more than one million persons charged with state felonies. *Gideon* established that an indigent person has the right to appointed counsel. Today, though, what quality of representation does that counsel provide?

This chapter discusses the current crisis in defense systems serving indigent clients and efforts to improve those systems. It analyzes the legal standard for adequate assistance of counsel and examines whether *Gideon*'s promise is being fulfilled by counsel and protected by the courts.

Crisis in Defense Systems

The present systems for providing indigent defense at the state level fail in many ways. Most commentators and bar leaders agree that the major factors contributing to poor quality of defense services are excessive caseloads, lack of funds for expert witnesses and investigators, and extremely low pay rates. These factors contribute to defense systems in which clients rarely see their lawyers. Some clients are simply processed through the system, receiving what some have called "assembly-line justice." In response to these failures, a growing number of lawsuits seek systemic changes at the state level.

One of the first cases aimed at realizing *Gideon's* promise through systemic litigation was *State v. Peart*, 621 So. 2d 780 (La. 1993). The Louisiana Supreme Court found that due to "excessive caseloads and the insufficient support with which their [public defender] attorneys must work, indigent defendants in [New Orleans] are generally not provided with effective assistance of counsel." (*Id.* at 789.) Finding the quality of defense services lacking, the Louisiana Supreme Court adopted "a rebuttable presumption" that the indigent defendants in New Orleans were "receiving assistance of counsel not sufficiently effective to meet constitutionally required standards." (*Id.* at 791.) This rebuttable presumption placed the burden on the state to prove that defense counsel was effective before the trial judge could permit a case awaiting trial to proceed. Not surprisingly, the ruling prompted the Louisiana legislature to increase spending on indigent defense in order to remove this presumption of ineffective assistance.

In a case dealing with contracts awarded to private attorneys, the Supreme Court of Arizona held that an indigent defense system operating on a flat fee bidding system, regardless of the number or type of cases, created a presumption of ineffective assistance of counsel. (*State v. Smith*, 681 P.2d 1374 (Ariz. 1984).) In another case, the New York County Lawyer's Association successfully sued for a preliminary injunction to increase the hourly fees for indigent defense lawyers in New York City, and the court held that the fee schedule resulted in ineffective assistance counsel. (*New York County Lawyers Ass'n v. State*, 745 N.Y.S.2d 376 (Sup. Ct. 2002).)

The states of Mississippi, Pennsylvania, South Dakota, Utah, and Wyoming do not contribute funds for indigent defense except in capital cases. They rely on counties to fund indigent defense for noncapital cases. In Mississippi, one county unsuccessfully sued seeking a declaratory judgment that the state's failure to contribute funding toward indigent defense in noncapital cases led to systemic ineffective assistance of counsel. In *Quitman County Miss. v. State*, 910 So. 2d 1032 (Miss. 2005), the Mississippi Supreme Court affirmed a circuit court decision denying declaratory judgment, reasoning that the county had failed to produce sufficient evidence of specific examples of the public defenders' legal representation falling below the objective standard of professional reasonableness. (*Id.* at 1037.)

Lawsuits seeking smaller caseloads or more pay have met with success in Arizona, Connecticut, Oklahoma, and Pennsylvania. Similar cases are pending in several other states.

In addition to issues of underfunding and overworking defense counsel, many believe that the current legal standard for adequate assistance of counsel does little to ensure that indigent clients receive competent representation.

Constitutional Standard for Adequate Assistance of Counsel

Ten years after *Gideon* was decided, Judge Bazelon, writing for a panel of the U.S. Court of Appeals for the District of Columbia Circuit, stated that effective assistance of counsel means "a defendant is entitled to the reasonably competent assistance of an attorney acting as his diligent conscientious advocate." (*United States v. DeCoster*, 487 F.2d 1197, 1202 (D.C. Cir. 1973).) Judge Bazelon's decision held that courts should measure the competency of defense counsel according to the ABA Standards for Criminal Justice, and, upon finding a substantial violation of any of the standards, the burden of proof should be on the government to show lack of prejudice to the defendant. (*Id.* at 1204.) Judge Bazelon reasoned that shifting the burden to the government to prove lack of prejudice was necessary for two reasons: first, the government has the burden of proving guilt, and requiring a defendant to prove prejudice would be tantamount to requiring the defendant to prove innocence, and second, "proof of prejudice may well be absent from the record precisely because counsel has been ineffective." (*Id.*) The decision pointed out that many failures to act, such as failure to investigate the case, interview witnesses, or call witnesses, are absent from the record when counsel renders inadequate assistance. (*Id.*)

Some federal circuits followed Judge Bazelon's approach, whereas other federal circuits required the defendant to show prejudice when making an ineffective assistance of counsel claim. In *Strickland v. Washington*, 466 U.S. 668, 687 (1984), the Supreme Court settled the debate by holding that Sixth Amendment ineffective assistance of counsel claims require the defendant to prove two elements: first, objectively unreasonable performance by the lawyer, and second, prejudice—a reasonable probability that the lawyer's inadequate performance adversely affected the outcome of the case. This standard, particularly the requirement that the lawyer's inadequate performance must be proven to have adversely affected the outcome of the case, is, as Judge Bazelon opined, a very difficult, at times impossible, standard to meet when counsel has provided inadequate representation.

This prejudice requirement is supported by a number of pragmatic concerns. It reflects a realist view that lawyers cannot perform perfectly in every trial. It also avoids spending time and money on a second trial likely to arrive at the same result as the first trial. There is also a strong interest in finality of judgments. One finds similar requirements in the Federal Rules of Evidence and the Federal Rules of Criminal Procedure. For example, the "harmless error" standard provides that erroneous rulings admitting or excluding evidence will not trigger reversal unless there is a showing that a "substantial right of the party is affected." (FED. R. EVID. 103; *see also* FED. R. CRIM. PROC. 52(a) (stating that any error "that does not affect substantial rights must be disregarded").)

But such a prejudice requirement also raises a number of serious concerns. If no prejudice is found, poor lawyering is left unremedied when a new trial is denied. This fact undermines incapacitation, as well as specific and general deterrence of incompetent lawyers, and erodes the faith of the defendant and the public in the fairness and integrity of our criminal justice system. A prejudice requirement also assumes we can accurately assess after the fact the impact of bad lawyering on the outcome of a case. Such an assessment can be quite difficult. If the lawyer failed to conduct an investigation, for example, how is one to know after the fact what the investigation would have turned up and how it would have affected the outcome of the case?

The Supreme Court does not always insist on a showing of prejudice in order to grant a new trial based on a constitutional violation. For example, the Court has held that reversal is necessary even without a showing of prejudice in some conflict of interest situations "when the trial court has failed to make an inquiry even when it knows or reasonably should know that a particular [client-attorney] conflict exists." (*Wood v. Georgia*, 450 U.S. 261, 272 (1981).) Should the Court similarly dispense with a prejudice requirement in the area of incompetent representation? Such an approach would address the difficulty the prejudice requirement poses for the defendant when there are failures to act by defense counsel that are absent from the record. Abandoning the prejudice requirement might also send a powerful message to those responsible for providing counsel to take measures to address the issue of quality of representation.

If there is going to be a prejudice requirement, who should bear the burden of proof? Should it be on the defendant? Or should the prosecution bear the burden of proving lack of prejudice to the defendant once there has been a finding of incompetent representation? Placing the burden on the prosecution to prove lack of prejudice, as Judge Bazelon did in *DeCoster*, would emphasize the accused's right to competent representation. Except when there is overwhelming evidence of guilt, however, prosecutors would face the same difficulty of proving lack of prejudice that defendants currently face in proving prejudice.

Placing the burden of proof to show prejudice on the defendant requires the defendant to rely on a record that may not reveal all of the instances of defense counsel's poor performance, such as the failure to investigate the case, call witnesses, or present scientific evidence that may negate evidence presented by the prosecution. Compounding this problem is the fact that defendants must prove incompetence and prejudice in postconviction relief hearings in which *Gideon* does not guarantee them the right to lawyers. As a result, only the most egregious instances of ineffective assistance of counsel apparent from the trial record lead to reversals.

The ABA's Ten Principles

Lack of confidence in the quality of defense services nationwide prompted the ABA House of Delegates to adopt "Ten Principles of a Public Defense Delivery System," recommended by the ABA Standing Committee on Legal Aid and Indigent Defendants. The principles state that a public defense delivery system must contain the elements described in the principles in order to deliver effective, efficient, high-quality, ethical, and conflict-free representation. The principles address the needs for manageable workloads, resource parity between defense and prosecution, continuity of representation so that the same lawyer represents a client from initial assignment through the trial and sentencing, continuing legal education for defense counsel, and systematic reviews and supervision of defense counsel to ensure quality of representation. (*Id.*)

Former ABA President Robert E. Hirshon stated that the Ten Principles present "the fundamental criteria for an adequate public defender system." Since their adoption, the Ten Principles have figured prominently in efforts to improve indigent defense systems in several states. In Texas, the Ten Principles are being used to develop and enforce uniform standards for indigent defense systems in every county. In Montana, lawyers bringing a class action lawsuit against the state and seven counties are arguing that the defense services in those counties are constitutionally deficient and do not meet any of the Ten Principles. The Michigan State Bar voted to adopt the Ten Principles, and the Georgia Supreme Court Commission on Indigent Defense recently used the Ten Principles as the focal point for a conference devoted to indigent defense standards and attributes of quality indigent defense systems.

Conclusion

In writing the *Gideon* decision for a unanimous Court, Justice Hugo Black stated, "[L]awyers in criminal cases are necessities, not luxuries." (*Gideon*, 372 U.S. at 344.) More than forty years after *Gideon*, too many indigent defendants are finding that it is still a luxury to have a competent lawyer. The Ten Principles provide a useful road map for designing effective defense systems. Courts and legislatures should adopt them as a yardstick for measuring whether defense systems are protecting the constitutional rights of clients and ensuring that defense counsel are fulfilling their ethical obligations to clients. Until indigent defense systems consistently provide the accused with lawyers who are able to comply with the legal standard for adequate representation of counsel, as well as the ethical standard for competency, the promise of *Gideon* will remain unfulfilled.

Resources for Chapter 4

Rules and Standards

FEDERAL RULE OF CRIMINAL PROCEDURE 52(a).
FEDERAL RULE OF EVIDENCE 103.

Cases and Ethics Opinions

Gideon v. Wainwright, 372 U.S. 335 (1963).
United States v. DeCoster, 487 F.2d 1197 (D.C. Cir. 1973).
Wood v. Georgia, 450 U.S. 261 (1981).
Strickland v. Washington, 466 U.S. 668 (1984).
State v. Smith, 681 P.2d 1374 (Ariz. 1984).
State v. Peart, 621 So. 2d 780 (La. 1993).
New York County Lawyers Ass'n v. State, 745 N.Y.S.2d 376 (Sup. Ct. 2002).
Quitman County Miss. v. State, 910 So. 2d 1032 (Miss. 2005).

Articles, Reports, Books, and Other Sources

Yale Kamisar et al., *Facing the Crisis, Fulfilling the Promise*, 41 AM. CRIM. L. REV. 135 (2004).

Robert E. Hirshon, *"Ten Principles" Are Key to Creating and Improving Public Defense Systems*.

ABA Standing Committee on Legal Aid and Indigent Defendants, TEN PRINCIPLES OF A PUBLIC DEFENSE DELIVERY SYSTEM (February 2002), *available at* http://www.abanet.org/legalservices/downloads/sclaid/indigentdefense/tenprinciplesbooklet.pdf.

CHAPTER 5

Inadequate Representation and Wrongful Convictions

DNA testing has demonstrated that our criminal justice system convicts an alarming number of innocent people. In almost every state, the number of wrongful convictions revealed continues to grow. Even these numbers fail to capture the full scope of the problem because DNA testing is capable of revealing inaccuracy only in cases in which the police obtain evidence—such as blood, semen, or hair—that can be submitted for DNA testing. Because the causes of wrongful conviction are not restricted to such cases, there is reason to believe that an even greater number of wrongful convictions occur in the many cases in which DNA testing cannot be used.

The subject of wrongful conviction has received national attention in recent years. This chapter considers how ineffective assistance by defense lawyers contributes to wrongful convictions.

Causes of Wrongful Convictions

Research reveals a constellation of causes for wrongful convictions. Mistaken eyewitness identification is a leading factor, along with police and prosecutorial misconduct, false confessions, unreliable informants, faulty scientific evidence, and racial bias. Unfortunately, inadequate representation by defense counsel has also been revealed as a major contributing cause.

Just as wrongful convictions are linked to a variety of factors, including bad lawyering, one can trace bad lawyering, in turn, to another group of factors. Professor Adele Bernhard identifies several of these in her contribution to the book *Wrongfully Convicted:*

When Justice Fails. (Adele Bernhard, *Effective Assistance of Counsel*, in WRONGLY CONVICTED: WHEN JUSTICE FAILS 220 (Saundra Westervelt & John Humphrey eds. 2001).) Quality control mechanisms for defense lawyers are lacking in part because of the difficulty in defining what constitutes good lawyering in the criminal defense context. In addition to definitional problems, enforcement is also problematic. The restrictive *Strickland* standard for reversal on the basis of ineffective assistance—requiring "a reasonable probability that, but for counsel's unprofessional errors, the result of the proceeding would have been different"—allows most bad lawyering to go unremedied and undeterred by the grant of a new trial. Similarly, malpractice standards in criminal cases effectively insulate bad lawyering from monetary disincentives. A convicted defendant must prove factual innocence to sustain a malpractice claim against a criminal defense lawyer in most states, and some states insulate public defenders entirely from civil lawsuits by former clients through governmental immunity.

The pressure to cooperate with prosecutors and judges generated by our criminal justice system's reliance on plea bargaining also discourages vigorous advocacy. More than 90 percent of criminal cases end in guilty pleas, and criminal defense lawyers often bargain repeatedly with the same prosecutors in cases before the same judges. Many defense counsel work on a high volume of cases in a culture of compromise that tends to assume rather than question a defendant's guilt. The need to obtain concessions from prosecutors in such an environment pressures defense lawyers not to vigorously challenge guilt, police or prosecutor conduct, or the reliability of confessions and eyewitness identifications. Some commentators describe the dynamics of negotiating guilty pleas as turning many defense lawyers into "double agents" who pressure or "con" defendants to plead guilty instead of thoroughly investigating cases and zealously representing their clients.

Inadequate funding also contributes to bad lawyering. Lack of funds makes it difficult for those charged with crimes to retain good lawyers and for lawyers to give adequate time to preparing cases. Shortage of funds also poses a barrier to gaining help from investigators and forensic experts. The large caseloads of appointed counsel and public defenders exacerbate these problems.

Ethical Dimensions of Inadequate Representation

The ethical shortcomings of inadequate representation are obvious. Lawyers are ethically bound to provide competent representation.

Model Rule of Professional Conduct 1.1 "requires the legal knowledge, skill, thoroughness and preparation reasonably necessary for the representation." Lawyers also have a duty of diligence that requires them to "take whatever lawful and ethical means are required to vindicate a client's cause." (MODEL RULE OF PROF'L CONDUCT 1.3 cmt. [1].) Diligence also requires that a "lawyer's work-load . . . be controlled so that each matter can be handled competently." (MODEL RULE 1.3 cmt. [2].) The limited resources of many defendants who hire private lawyers, the chronic underpayment of appointed counsel, and the underfunding of public defender services mean that lawyers are unlikely to meet these ethical commands simply because they do not have the time or resources to do so. The stringent standards for reversal in *Strickland* and for malpractice liability also create little incentive for defense lawyers to meet their ethical obligations.

In addition to undermining adherence to ethical obligations of competence and diligence, inequality in resources undermines in a broader sense the functioning of the entire adversary system that underlies and is used to justify many procedural and ethical rules in criminal practice. The adversary system assumes each side has the resources with which to discover and demonstrate the legal and factual strengths of its position and the legal and factual weaknesses of its opponent's position. As the two sides present their cases and challenge those of their opponent, the strength or weakness of that showing in theory should reflect the merits of their positions. But if one side lacks resources to investigate, prepare, and present its case and challenge its opponent's case, then the weakness in its showing and its inability to challenge the opponent may have little to do with the merits. It may simply reflect lack of resources.

West Virginia's investigation of Fred Zain, as described by Professor Paul Giannelli, illustrates the insidious effect lack of defense resources may have on the adversary system. (Paul Giannelli, *The Abuse of Scientific Evidence in Criminal Cases: The Need for Independent Crime Laboratories,* 4 VA. J. SOC. POL'Y & L. 439 (1997).) The head serologist at the West Virginia State Police crime laboratory, Zain was a prosecution witness against Glen Dale Woodall in a double rape case. Zain testified at trial that Woodall's blood type matched that of the assailant. Woodall was convicted and sentenced to a long term of imprisonment in 1987. Five years later, DNA testing exonerated Woodall of the rapes and led to an investigation of Zain. That investigation revealed that Zain had falsified test results in as many as 134 cases from 1979 to 1989.

Zain's typical modus operandi was to falsify his tests to confirm the prosecution's theory of the crime.

How, one might well ask, could Zain have gotten away with such falsification in so many cases? Why would he have the temerity to try to falsify so many test results? The adversary system's classic response to false testimony is to subject it to the rigors of cross-examination and counterproof. Zain's testimony in theory should have been exposed by rigorous cross-examination and counterproof by defense experts. The fear of such exposure should have deterred Zain from even attempting such falsification. But Zain had little reason to fear. Lack of resources for expert witnesses is a chronic problem in defense representation and, without such resources, neither rigorous cross-examination nor counterproof keep prosecution experts honest.

Zain, in theory, was operating in an adversary system that should have provided powerful checks against false testimony. In fact, he was operating in a system that relied entirely on forensic testimony from only one side: the government. This imbalance in resources is hidden from public view by a preoccupation with high-profile cases, such as the O.J. Simpson case, in which wealthy defendants have access to lawyers well versed in forensic science and experts who can match those presented by the government. The same is not true for defendants who lack resources.

Remedying the Imbalance of Resources

How can we remedy the imbalance in resources that undermines effective representation and the fairness and accuracy of the criminal justice system? One measure that has been called for by critics of the criminal justice system is to provide defendants with greater resources. Shortages in state budgets, the hardening of public attitudes toward criminals, and the fact that the inadequacy of defense resources has been pointed out repeatedly for years without remedy suggest that this avenue does not hold much promise. Perhaps, though, the notoriety and concern generated by the wave of recent DNA exonerations will lead to change.

If more defense resources are not forthcoming, another remedial avenue would be to concede that we lack a functioning adversary system in areas such as forensic evidence and move toward a more cooperative model. If the defense regularly lacks resources to hire forensic experts, we could institute structural changes to transform the stance of the government's expert from that of a partisan witness allied with the prosecution to a more neutral posture. One way to do this would be to make government experts more independent of the prosecution than they currently are. Under such a redesigned system, crime labs would no longer be allied with the police and prosecutors but would be independent entities functioning under the supervision of the state or federal courts. Scientific standards, including standards for personnel qualifications, could be established, and safeguards for reliability, such as blind testing and the use of protocols, could be adopted.

Except in rare instances when good cause and a scientific basis for doing so are demonstrated, the forensic personnel working in these labs would no longer be given information about who the police "think" committed the offense. Instead, forensic personnel would rely on blind testing free from potentially biasing input and influence of police and prosecutors. If the prosecution wished to hire consulting or testimonial experts separate and apart from those affiliated with an independent crime lab, it would be barred from doing so unless equal funds were made available to the defense for the same purpose.

Conclusion

The mounting number of wrongful convictions has shed light on serious flaws in our criminal justice system. DNA testing demonstrates that defendants, who are most often poor, are vulnerable to erroneous conviction through mistaken identification, false confession, unreliable informants, police and prosecutorial misconduct, racial bias, and faulty scientific evidence. Inadequate representation provided by overworked and underfunded defense lawyers greatly enhances that vulnerability. Though elimination of the risk of erroneous conviction may not be possible, recognizing and responding to the realities of criminal defense practice could greatly reduce that risk. If the right to counsel for criminal defendants is to have any real meaning, we must take steps to remedy the gross imbalance between prosecution and defense in representation and resources. If we fail to take such steps, our system will continue to convict far too many who are innocent.

Resources for Chapter 5

Rules and Standards

MODEL RULES OF PROFESSIONAL CONDUCT 1.1 and 1.3.

Articles, Reports, Books, and Other Sources

Abraham S. Blumberg, *The Practice of Law as a Confidence Game: Organizational Cooptation of a Profession*, 1 LAW & SOC'Y REV. 15 (1967).

Paul C. Giannelli, *The Abuse of Scientific Evidence in Criminal Cases: The Need for Independent Crime Laboratories*, 4 VA. J. SOC. POL'Y & L. 439 (1997).

Rodney Uphoff, *Convicting the Innocent: Aberration or Systemic Problem?*, 2006 WIS. L. REV. 739.

Adele Bernhard, *Effective Assistance of Counsel*, in WRONGLY CONVICTED: WHEN JUSTICE FAILS 220 (Saundra Westervelt & John Humphrey eds. 2001).

PART 3

Criminal Practice and the Media

CHAPTER 6

Trial by Media: Arguing Cases in the Court of Public Opinion

Prosecutors and defense lawyers have often sought to use the media to shape public opinion and tilt the scales of justice. Courts and the bar have attempted to check these efforts by regulating publicity in ways that balance the competing interests of a fair trial, free speech, and the public's right to be informed.

On the one hand, traditions of free speech and the role of lawyers as zealous advocates have led the courts and bar authorities to acknowledge that in some instances comments to the press or others outside of the courtroom are necessary to protect the rights of the client. On the other hand, the concept of lawyers as officers of the court supports regulations limiting extrajudicial comments so that the right to a fair trial and orderly administration of justice are protected.

This chapter discusses the policy debate, history, and current ethics rules concerning public comment by lawyers. It also identifies some areas of ambiguity in the law and ethics rules regulating lawyers advocating in the court of public opinion.

Should Public Comment by Lawyers Be Regulated?

For a variety of reasons, the danger publicity poses to legal proceedings has been a long-standing concern.

Protecting Trials

Our criminal justice system is premised on the view that jurors and judges should resolve cases free from the direct influence of public opinion. In an early trial publicity case, Justice Holmes stated, "The theory of our system is that the conclusions to be reached in a case will be induced by evidence and argument in open court, and not by any outside influence, whether of private talk or public print." (*Patterson v. Colorado*, 205 U.S. 454, 462 (1907).) Under this view, jurors are to decide cases based solely on the information they learn at trial—information that satisfies evidence rules and has been subjected to trial guarantees of trustworthiness such as oath and cross-examination. Publicity surrounding a trial increases the risk that jurors will decide cases based on information learned outside the courtroom that is untrustworthy or inadmissible.

Our system is also premised on the view that jurors should decide cases based on the applicable law. Publicity creates a risk that the jurors' verdict will conform to public sentiment rather than the law.

The fairness of a trial also depends on judges making decisions based on the law and information they obtain through a litigation process that gives both sides equal opportunity to present information and to respond to information presented by an opponent. Public comment may generate publicity that pressures a judge to ignore the law if it requires him or her to render an unpopular decision. It may also give the judge information unfavorable to one party without that party having an opportunity to comment and respond.

Witness testimony is the primary source of evidence in our trial system. Publicity may make witnesses hesitant to come forward or to testify, particularly if they feel their testimony may help an unpopular defendant. Witnesses who do testify may consciously conform their testimony to what they learn through publicity, or unconsciously conflate their original perceptions with what they learn through the public comment of lawyers.

The lawyers representing the parties present a particular danger to the functioning of jurors, judges, and witnesses because prosecutors and defense lawyers are likely to have access to inadmissible information, such as a defendant's confession or refusal to take a lie detector test, or the prior sexual conduct of a complainant. Public comment by a prosecutor may also damage the due process rights of a defendant by airing information about the defendant that would be inadmissible at trial and inflame potential juror prejudices.

Protecting Clients

Regulating public comment by lawyers may also protect clients. The public comments of a lawyer could damage a client in various ways. The lawyer may reveal confidential information, disclose strategy, or make a statement that could later be used as an evidentiary admission. Public comment might lead the lawyer to take an early strategic position (such as mistaken identity or self-defense) without complete information, only to be forced to abandon that position later with a consequent loss of both lawyer and client credibility.

The lawyer's own desire for notoriety may improperly influence a decision to engage in public comment. The notion that "any press is good press as long as they spell my name correctly" illustrates the incentive that could prompt a lawyer to create media attention for the purpose of generating new legal business, increasing name recognition for possible elected office, or simply for ego gratification.

Although public comment poses risks of harming the client, cutting against a ban on lawyer public comment is the fact that it may be necessary to protect a client's reputation. When a person is charged, the state is saying that it believes the defendant is guilty. If the defense lawyer fails to comment, the public may interpret the defense lawyer's silence as an admission of guilt. In addition, if publicity is likely to affect jurors, the judge, and witnesses, then a lawyer's failure to comment and present the client's side may have the effect of ensuring that the publicity the case receives is skewed unfairly against the client.

Protecting the Public

When lawyers who represent the parties engage in public comment, they are under great pressure to "spin" the facts and law favorably to their clients. This creates great risk that they will distort the facts and law in a way that misinforms the public. The public has an interest in being informed, but that interest is not served when the lawyers' comments misinform the public. For example, Arthur Andersen set up a public Web site urging an end to a criminal investigation of its activities relating to Enron and posted a background paper prepared by its lawyers asserting "factual and legal errors" in the government's case. As Professor Kathleen Brickey has demonstrated, that paper was inaccurate and misleading on a number of points. (Kathleen F. Brickey, *Andersen's Fall from Grace*, 81 WASH. U. L.Q. 917 (2003).)

Lawyers who do not represent the parties are typically free to comment on pending cases and thus are available to inform the public about the legal issues in the case without having a fiduciary responsibility to a client or an interest in spinning the facts or law. Today, most TV networks have stables of expert legal commentators who can describe and explain the law without creating the risks generated by having the lawyers who represent the parties comment.

History of Ethics Regulation

Alabama adopted the first lawyer ethics code in 1887. It advised against statements to the press, and this principle appeared in the ABA's first set of ethics rules, the 1908 ABA Canons of Ethics. Canon 20 provided, "Newspaper publications by a lawyer as to the merits of pending or anticipated litigation may interfere with a fair trial in the Courts and otherwise prejudice the due administration of justice. Generally they are to be condemned." Canon 20 recognized that "extreme circumstances" might justify publication, but that it was "unprofessional to make it anonymously." Although these early ethics rules discouraged extrajudicial comments, they were vague and rarely enforced.

Through the first half of the twentieth century, cases such as the Sacco and Vanzetti murder trial and the Lindbergh kidnapping trial attracted great publicity, raising questions of whether intensive media coverage largely unfavorable to the defendants influenced jury verdicts. In *Sheppard v. Maxwell*, 384 U.S. 333 (1966), Doctor Sam Sheppard was convicted in a highly publicized trial of murdering his wife. The Court reversed his conviction finding that publicity in the case was prejudicial. The prosecution and law enforcement officials repeatedly made information available to the media that was not admissible evidence at trial, such as Sheppard's refusal to take a lie detector test and a report that there was a "bombshell witness on tap." (*Id.* at 360–61.) The Court noted that the press publicized gossip as "evidence" and that statements by Sheppard, his family, and his lawyers to the press compounded the problem. The *Sheppard* case established the standard that when there is a "reasonable likelihood that prejudicial news prior to trial will prevent a fair trial," the judge should take steps such as "continuing the trial, changing venue, or sequestering the jury." (*Id.* at 363.) In extreme cases, a new trial should be ordered. The Court also made clear that a statement by counsel "affecting the fairness of a criminal trial is not only subject to regulation, but is highly censurable and worthy of disciplinary measures." (*Id.*)

Prior to *Sheppard,* out-of-court statements by lawyers concerning pending matters were usually regulated by the First Amendment "clear and present danger" test to justify the prior restraint of speech. The shift in *Sheppard* to the standard of "reasonable likelihood" of prejudicing a fair trial signaled a lower First Amendment protection for lawyer speech. In the wake of *Sheppard,* both the ABA and the states reevaluated their ethics rules and many imposed specific restrictions on lawyer public comment.

Twenty-five years after *Sheppard,* the Supreme Court in *Gentile v. Nevada State Bar,* 501 U.S. 1030 (1991), explicitly confronted whether extrajudicial speech by a lawyer must pose a "clear and present danger" to a legal proceeding to justify a disciplinary sanction, or whether a lesser standard suffices. Dominic Gentile represented a storage facility owner charged with stealing drugs police had stored as evidence, and the case drew a great deal of publicity prior to an indictment. (*Id.* at 1039.) Immediately after the indictment was issued, Gentile held a press conference to counter adverse publicity about his client. He asserted his client's innocence, impugned the motives of some prosecution witnesses, and suggested that some police officers might be responsible for the theft. (*Id.* at 1045.) The Nevada Supreme Court affirmed a state bar disciplinary board recommendation that Gentile receive a private reprimand based on a Nevada rule that prohibited statements "substantially likely" to prejudice a proceeding. A closely divided U.S. Supreme Court overturned the discipline on vagueness grounds but upheld the "substantially likely" standard. (*Id.* at 1048, 1063.)

Current Ethics Rules Regulating Pretrial and Trial Publicity

Subsequent to *Gentile,* the ABA and several states modified their ethics rules to provide more guidance and to rebalance the First Amendment rights of lawyers, the defendant's right to a fair trial, and the public's right to information. The current version of Model Rule 3.6, followed by most states, restricts a lawyer "who is participating or has participated in the investigation or litigation of a matter" from making out-of-court statements that the lawyer "knows or reasonably should know" will be publicly disseminated and "will have a substantial likelihood of materially prejudicing" a proceeding in the matter. Thus, lawyers involved in a case may not make statements calculated to influence the adjudication of a matter. Model Rule 3.6 does not apply to lawyers not participating in the investigation or litigation of the case.

Model Rule 3.6 states seven classes of information that a lawyer may publicly state in a criminal case:

(1) the claim, offense or defense involved and, except when prohibited by law, the identity of the persons involved;
(2) information contained in a public record;
(3) that an investigation of a matter is in progress;
(4) the scheduling or result of any step in litigation;
(5) a request for assistance in obtaining evidence or information necessary thereto;
(6) a warning of danger concerning the behavior of a person involved, when there is reason to believe that there exists the likelihood of substantial harm to an individual or to the public interest; and
(7) in a criminal case, in addition to paragraphs (1) through (6):
    (i) the identity, residence, occupation and family status of the accused;
    (ii) if the accused has not been apprehended, information necessary to aid in the apprehension of that person;
    (iii) the fact, time and place of arrest; and
    (iv) the identity of investigating and arresting officers or agencies and the length of the investigation.

Comment [5] to Model Rule 3.6 identifies six categories of statements that are "more likely than not to have material prejudicial effect on a proceeding, particularly when they refer to a civil matter triable to a jury, a criminal matter, or any other proceeding that could result in incarceration":

(1) the character, credibility, reputation or criminal record of a party, suspect in a criminal investigation or witness, or the identity of a witness, or the expected testimony of a party or witness;
(2) in a criminal case or proceeding that could result in incarceration, the possibility of a plea of guilty to the offense or the existence or contents of any confession, admission, or statement given by a defendant or suspect or that person's refusal or failure to make a statement;
(3) the performance or results of any examination or test or the refusal or failure of a person to submit to an examination or test, or the identity or nature of physical evidence expected to be presented;

(4) any opinion as to the guilt or innocence of a defendant or suspect in a criminal case or proceeding that could result in incarceration;
(5) information that the lawyer knows or reasonably should know is likely to be inadmissible as evidence in a trial and that would, if disclosed, create a substantial risk of prejudicing an impartial trial; or
(6) the fact that a defendant has been charged with a crime, unless there is included therein a statement explaining that the charge is merely an accusation and the defendant is presumed innocent until and unless proven guilty.

In addition to the categories of acceptable and unacceptable extrajudicial statements, Model Rule 3.6 contains a fair reply clause that permits a lawyer to "make a statement that a reasonable lawyer would believe is required to protect a client from substantial undue prejudicial effect of recent publicity not initiated by the lawyer or the lawyer's client" provided the statement is "limited to such information as is necessary to mitigate the recent adverse publicity."

Prosecutors must follow Model Rule 3.6 and also have a special responsibility under Model Rule 3.8(f) to "refrain from making extrajudicial comments that have a substantial likelihood of heightening public condemnation of the accused and exercise reasonable care to prevent investigators, law enforcement personnel, employees or other persons assisting or associated with the prosecutor in a criminal case from making an extrajudicial statement that the prosecutor would be prohibited from making under Rule 3.6 or this Rule."

In addition to Model Rules 3.6 and 3.8, Model Rule 8.4 states that it is professional misconduct for a lawyer to "knowingly assist or induce another" to violate a Rule of Professional Conduct. Thus, neither a prosecutor nor defense lawyer may enlist others to disseminate information prohibited by Rule 3.6.

Borderline Issues

The trials of Martha Stewart and Arthur Andersen illustrate a phenomenon of clients waging media campaigns to influence the government and to sway public opinion. In both cases, the clients engaged public relations firms and sought to pressure the government not to prosecute. In addition to issuing press releases, both

Stewart and Andersen argued for their innocence on Web sites. In both instances, their lawyers appeared to play some role in shaping the public message that coincided with the legal positions to be taken if the cases reached court. But the extrajudicial speech was usually that of the clients and not the lawyers. What role may lawyers play in such media campaigns without violating ethical public comment restrictions? Courts and ethics authorities have yet to address this question, and we explore a lawyer's involvement in client media campaigns in Chapter 8.

Another borderline issue is the use of pleadings to reveal matters protected by the ethics rules on public comment. For example, some defense lawyers have revealed in motions or other pretrial filings the prior sexual or mental histories of complainants, knowing that this material will likely be inadmissible but will find its way into the press. Similarly, some prosecutors have used court filings to reveal the prior criminal history and uncharged bad acts of defendants.

Prosecutors have an ethical duty to prevent law enforcement and others associated with the prosecution from making statements the prosecutor cannot make. But many high-profile cases involve "leaks" of information protected by the ethics rules on public comment. Defense lawyers do not have a corresponding ethical duty to prevent clients from talking with the press, and it is not clear that imposing such a duty would be valid under the First Amendment.

Conclusion

Silence is typically the safest policy for protecting a client from harm and a lawyer from discipline or sanctions. But prosecutors and defense counsel at times have to decide whether speaking to the media is ethically permissible and in the interests of their clients, for example, to counter statements by the press, law enforcement officials, or opposing counsel. When faced with such a decision, lawyers need to weigh the potential risks and rewards carefully.

Resources for Chapter 6

Rules and Standards

Model Rules of Professional Conduct 3.6, 3.8(f), and 8.4.
ABA Canons of Ethics, Canon 20.

Cases and Ethics Opinions

Patterson v. Colorado, 205 U.S. 454 (1907).
Sheppard v. Maxwell, 384 U.S. 333 (1966).
Gentile v. Nevada State Bar, 501 U.S. 1030 (1991).

Articles, Reports, Books, and Other Sources

Erwin Chemerinsky, *Lawyers Have Free Speech Rights, Too: Why Gag Orders on Trial Participants Are Almost Always Unconstitutional*, 17 LOY. L.A. ENT. L. REV. 311 (1997).

Kathleen F. Brickey, *Andersen's Fall From Grace*, 81 WASH. U. L.Q. 917 (2003).

CHAPTER 7

Clients, Lawyers, and the Media

Media scrutiny of criminal trials is commonplace. Newspapers give extensive attention to criminal trials of celebrities such as Martha Stewart and those, such as Scott Peterson, accused of terrible crimes. And television, through Court TV, provides coverage and commentary on criminal trials of even obscure defendants. The lawyer and the client have limited ability to control print or television coverage, which is usually limited to what an observer sitting in the courtroom would see. The Constitution requires public criminal trials, and newspapers and television cameras extend public access to open courtroom proceedings beyond the relatively small number of spectators a typical courtroom holds.

Some cases, though, demonstrate that television may be poised to expand the scope and intrusiveness of its coverage of criminal trials, raising challenging questions of legal ethics.

Access to the Jury Room

The State of Texas charged Cedric Harrison with murder and sought capital punishment. Prior to trial, Harrison consented to the PBS documentary series *Frontline* videotaping the jury deliberations in his case for later broadcast. Though Harrison waived the right to use the video recording in any later challenge to a conviction, the prosecutor in the case opposed the recording. The trial judge held a hearing and questioned both Harrison and his lawyer about Harrison's decision to consent, then ruled to allow the recording. Jurors were to be screened and only those who consented to the taping were to sit on Harrison's jury.

The prosecutor sought immediate appellate review, and a Texas appellate court, in *Texas v. Poe*, 98 S.W.3d 194 (2003), granted mandamus prohibiting the videotaping, finding that it violated a Texas statute providing that "[n]o person shall be permitted to be with a jury while it is deliberating." The court ostensibly adopted a textual approach to an interesting exercise in statutory interpretation. The cameras and microphones were to be remotely operated, so no person other than the jurors would have actually been in the jury room. The text of the statute simply did not address recording jury deliberations. Nonetheless, the court found that the plain language of the statute "clearly and indisputably" barred the recording. (*Id.* at 202.) According to the court, television viewers who would later watch the recording would be "with the jury while it is deliberating." (*Id.* at 201.) A more plausible rationale for the result reached by the court is one based on legislative purpose. The policy behind barring any person from being in the jury room may be seen as likewise dictating barring videotaping of the jury.

Should we allow the recording of jury deliberations? There are a number of persuasive arguments on both sides. We insist that criminal trials be public, but then shroud what is arguably the most crucial phase of the trial, the jury deciding the defendant's fate. Why doesn't the ideal that democratic government should be open dictate exposing jury deliberations to public view? Recording and broadcasting jury deliberations could help educate the public, legislators, and legal reformers about how juries operate and help us craft better procedure and evidence rules. It could also reveal and remedy jury misconduct, which in turn would arguably deter misconduct.

But how might such public exposure negatively affect the way jurors function? Jurors who conclude that the government has failed to prove the guilt of an unpopular defendant might nonetheless convict for fear of reprisal. They might also feel inhibited in freely expressing their views or in voting to nullify. Publicity might prompt some jurors to "act" for the cameras to gain notoriety for themselves, as do participants in reality television shows. The publicity resulting from such recording and broadcasting could also discourage potential jurors from serving, which would shrink and possibly skew the jury pool.

The debate about recording criminal jury deliberations has yet to be resolved. Though the Texas court in the *Harrison* case barred recording, Arizona, Ohio, Maine, and Wisconsin have allowed it. How other states will handle the issue remains to be seen.

Interviews with Clients and Recording Defense Preparation

Another case, *Echols v. Arkansas*, 127 S.W.3d 486 (Ark. 2003), raises a different aspect of media coverage beyond the typical courtroom broadcast. Arkansas prosecuted Echols and several codefendants for the gruesome murders of three young boys. The boys were found hog-tied in a drainage ditch. All had been sexually abused, and one was severely mutilated. Prior to trial, filmmakers under contract to HBO entered into an agreement with Echols and his two codefendants to interview them and film their trials in return for payments of $7,500 each. The defense lawyers did not receive any payments.

Echols was convicted and sentenced to death. In challenging his conviction, Echols raised an interesting argument: that his contract with the filmmakers created a conflict of interest for his trial lawyer that entitled him to a new trial. First, he argued that the lawyer sacrificed time meeting the needs of the filmmakers that should have been spent preparing for trial. Second, he argued that his lawyer chose to use the funds from the HBO contract to pay for investigation and expert witnesses rather than applying to the court for such funding, which might have been more ample. Finally, Echols argued that in order to accommodate the filmmakers' broadcast date, his lawyer failed to seek a continuance that could have helped the case.

The appellate court rejected each of these arguments because Echols failed to demonstrate an adverse impact on his lawyer's performance. The court also pointed out the advantages Echols received from the HBO agreement. For example, by using his own money rather than court funds for investigation and experts, his lawyer was able to prevent notification of the prosecution of the defense strategy that inevitably accompanies an application for court funds.

Lawyers Entering into Media Contracts

A lawyer negotiating a personal media deal is not an infrequent occurrence. Marcia Clark entered into a million-dollar contract to write a book about the O. J. Simpson case. One of the defense lawyers in that case, F. Lee Bailey, years before had negotiated a contract to write a book about his representation of Patricia Hearst, which gave rise to a claim of conflict of interest.

Such deals can create both constructive and perverse incentives for the lawyers who enter them. A book or television contract might reinforce the lawyer's incentives to be well prepared, diligent, and effective out of concern for reputation and to attract future clients. But the same contract may also threaten a number of ethical obligations. One of the most obvious is confidentiality. The financial incentives arising from such deals may also distort the lawyer's judgment about critical decisions such as acceptance of a guilty plea or choice of defense strategy, both of which might impact public interest in the case and thus its media value.

Courts and ethics committees have examined the ethics of lawyers entering into media deals on a number of occasions. Model Rule 1.8(d) reflects the approach typically taken by courts and ethics authorities regarding such deals. It states, "Prior to the conclusion of representation of a client, a lawyer shall not make or negotiate an agreement giving the lawyer literary or media rights to a portrayal or account based in substantial part on information relating to the representation." Comment [9] to Rule 1.8(d) explains the conflict by noting that "[m]easures suitable in the representation of the client may detract from the publication value of an account of the representation."

In short, lawyers are allowed to enter into a media deal as long as they wait until the representation is over. A moment's reflection reveals that this delay requirement does not insulate a lawyer from the perverse incentives such media deals create. The lawyer's conduct before and during a trial in a high-profile case may be distorted simply by the prospect of later entering into a media deal.

Client Media Deals and Lawyer Ethics

The *Harrison* and *Echols* cases raise an interesting set of ethical questions for lawyers. Who makes the decision? Rule 1.2 addresses the allocation between client and lawyer of the authority to make decisions concerning the representation. The client has final authority to make decisions concerning the objectives of the representation, whereas the lawyer has final authority over the means for pursuing those objectives. Rule 1.2 specifically states that what plea to enter, whether to waive jury trial, and whether to testify are questions for the client to resolve.

Are questions such as those faced by Harrison and Echols—whether to have jury deliberations recorded and whether to agree to a recorded interview—ultimately for the client or the lawyer to decide? Do these decisions concern objectives or strategy? In the

Harrison and *Echols* cases, both the lawyers and the courts appear to have assumed that these were client decisions. But are they? One could easily characterize both as questions of strategy. If the client and lawyer disagree on the strategic wisdom of enhanced media scrutiny, is the lawyer ethically allowed to veto a client's decision to agree to recording jury deliberations or granting an interview? Is the lawyer required to do so if the lawyer is convinced the publicity will hurt the client's case?

The lawyer may have little if any practical means of vetoing a client's decision to allow increased media access. The lawyer's veto power probably depends on the type of media exposure and whether the client is in custody. Clearly the lawyer could act to veto the recording of jury deliberations by opposing it in court. By contrast, the lawyer would be hard pressed to keep a client who is not in custody from granting an interview to a television crew.

Competent Representation

Model Rule 1.1 requires a lawyer to provide competent representation to a client. How does a lawyer decide whether or not enhanced media scrutiny will help or hurt the client? The lawyer confronts this issue regardless of whether the lawyer or the client makes the ultimate decision. If the decision is ultimately the client's to make, the lawyer nonetheless has to advise the client about which course is preferable. If the decision is ultimately the lawyer's to make, he or she similarly must determine which course is in the client's best interest.

Predicting whether and how enhanced media involvement will affect a client's case is likely to be a challenging and hazardous task. How is the lawyer to know, for example, whether recording jury deliberations will make the jury more or less likely to convict? Is a lawyer able to predict whether a jury pool screened of potential jurors uncomfortable with being taped will be more receptive or more hostile to the lawyer's arguments than an unscreened jury pool? The debate about recording jury deliberations reveals that questions such as these are hotly contested and not easily resolved. The fact that both sides make plausible claims suggests that such questions will be difficult for lawyers in individual cases to resolve. The *New York Times* ran a story detailing the testing done and the many experts consulted by Martha Stewart's legal team in planning a media campaign coordinated with her trial. How many lawyers will have access to such resources in deciding whether and how to have a client interact with the media?

Confidentiality

The taping of jury deliberations poses no apparent risk to confidentiality. But the agreement in *Echols* poses serious risks to confidentiality. The most obvious arises from the client being interviewed. Anything the client says is a potential admission, even if the client chooses not to testify at trial. And if the client does testify, statements made during the interview could be used for impeachment during cross-examination. Even if the interview is not broadcast until after the trial is over, the filmmakers and camera operators will know about the client's statements. If the prosecution is aware of the taping of such an interview, it might subpoena the film crew as well as its film or videotape. If there is a mistrial or a retrial after a reversal on appeal, the broadcast version could provide admissions and material for cross-examination at the retrial. If the filming includes defense strategy sessions, such as one mentioned in *Echols* about whether or not to call a certain witness, the film crew and its film or videotape provide potential avenues for such strategic information reaching the prosecution.

Conflict of Interest

Are the risks posed by scenarios such as the one in *Echols* serious enough to warrant a prophylactic approach? Or should courts simply look for evidence that such risks resulted in actual impairment of the lawyer's conduct or harm to the client's case?

As with lawyers themselves entering into media deals, the incentives here are mixed and courts will likely continue to take the second option and look for evidence that perverse incentives negatively affected the lawyer's conduct or harmed the client. But lawyers who find themselves in such situations should be aware of the risks those situations pose in order to guard against them.

Prosecutorial Objections

The prosecutor might have a number of reasons to object to enhanced media exposure in the form of recording jury deliberations for broadcast or a media deal by a defendant. First, the prosecutor may conclude that enhanced exposure would create a strategic disadvantage for the government. Second, the prosecution has an interest in eliminating grounds for possible appeal. The prosecutor also has an ethical duty to ensure that proceedings are fair to the defendant. Comment [1] to Rule 3.8 explains that the prosecutor has a "specific obligation to see that the defendant is accorded procedural justice, [and] that guilt is decided upon the basis of sufficient evidence. . . ." Finally, concern that perverse incentives created by a media deal may influence the defense lawyer's conduct may motivate the prosecutor to object.

A court is likely to give the prosecutor standing to object to the recording of jury deliberations, as the Texas trial and appellate courts did in the *Harrison* case. In fact, the prosecutor eventually prevailed and prevented the recording of jury deliberations in that case. It is less certain that a court would give a prosecutor any voice concerning media deals involving a defendant.

Conclusion

A lawyer's initial intuitive response might be that a client's agreement to increased media scrutiny poses no ethical risks for the lawyer. But the *Harrison* case and the ethical issues raised above show that such an assessment is faulty and that lawyers need to approach such situations with an awareness of the ethical risks they pose. Courts and legislators might also take note of those risks in deciding questions such as whether to allow the taping and broadcast of jury deliberations.

Resources for Chapter 7

Rules and Standards

Model Rules of Professional Conduct 1.1, 1.2, 1.8(d), and 3.8.

Cases and Ethics Opinions

Echols v. Arkansas, 127 S.W.3d 486 (Ark. 2003).
Texas v. Poe, 98 S.W.3d 194 (2003).

CHAPTER 8

The Role of Lawyers in Client Media Campaigns

Media campaigns to protect public images and fend off criminal liability are becoming increasingly popular among high-profile defendants. What role may a lawyer play in a client's media campaign? Ethics rules strictly govern the public comments of lawyers involved in investigating or litigating a case. Model Rule 3.6 bars such a lawyer from making "an extrajudicial statement that the lawyer knows or reasonably should know will be disseminated by means of public communication and will have a substantial likelihood of materially prejudicing an adjudicative proceeding in the matter." Lawyer ethics rules, though, obviously do not and cannot govern clients, most of whom are not lawyers. Unless the trial judge imposes a gag order, clients are free to speak about their cases if they choose to do so.

How should a lawyer operate in an environment in which the lawyer's speech is restricted but the client's is not? What ethics issues is the lawyer likely to face? One might initially think that because the client is speaking and not the lawyer, no legal ethics issues are raised. But closer examination reveals a number of challenging questions that client statements to the media present for the client's lawyer.

Rewards and Risks

To better understand these ethics issues, it is helpful to briefly canvass the potential rewards and risks of clients talking to the media during the investigation or trial of a criminal case.

Why do some clients choose to talk with the media? Surely, one motivation is to protect the client's reputation. Criminal investigations and charges routinely generate information, allegations, and rumors impugning the client. The public may interpret silence by the client as an admission that the negative things said about the client are true. The client may also hope that positive publicity generated by the client's statements may influence jurors, judges, witnesses, and perhaps even the prosecutor in ways favorable to the client.

Most lawyers, though, advise their clients not to talk to the press, and most clients heed that advice. Why? Public statements by a client might reveal confidential information and tip off the prosecutor to the defense's trial strategy. Public statements may also create evidentiary admissions and generate useful impeachment material for cross-examination, such as a prior inconsistent statement or a false exculpatory statement. In making an early statement, the client may take a strategic position based on imperfect information. If the defense later decides to change that position as more information is received from the prosecution or from the defense's own investigation, both client and lawyer may lose credibility.

Who Decides?

Who makes the decision whether or not a client should engage in a media campaign: the lawyer or the client? Model Rule 1.2 tells us that the objectives of the representation are for the client to decide but that the means for achieving them are for the lawyer to decide in consultation with the client. The question of whether the client should engage with the media prior to and during a trial certainly seems like a means decision for the lawyer. The media campaign appears to be a means to advance the objective of shielding the defendant from criminal punishment. But both the Model Rules and Supreme Court authority give the client final say over certain means or strategy decisions that have a constitutional dimension, such as whether or not to waive a jury trial or to testify. Because a client's decision to speak with the media implicates the client's First Amendment rights, one may argue that this decision should ultimately be the client's to make.

If the lawyer, in theory, has final say on this question, is there any practical way for the lawyer to keep the client from making a public statement? The lawyer can control what arguments are raised in an appellate brief because the lawyer writes and files the brief. Similarly, the lawyer has ultimate control over what matters are raised during cross-examination because the lawyer asks the questions during cross-examination. By contrast, the lawyer has no practical way to control whether a client, especially one not in custody, speaks to the media.

If the decision is the client's to make under Model Rule 1.2, most clients are likely to defer to their lawyers and effectively cede to them the power to make the decision. A wise lawyer will try to avoid having to confront this issue by talking it over with the client and reaching a decision both agree upon.

What if a client wants to make a public statement for a reason unrelated to winning the criminal case? A business executive charged with a crime, for example, might be motivated to minimize damage to future business interests even if a media campaign increases the risk of conviction. This choice, in our view, presents an objective of representation question for the client to decide. The defense lawyer is likely to place a very high value on minimizing risk of conviction and a relatively low value on a client's future business interests. This is so in part because the lawyer's professional training and competitive instincts lead the lawyer to focus almost exclusively on winning the case, and in part because the outcome of the case will influence the lawyer's reputation and future business interests. For these reasons, there is a risk the lawyer may be unresponsive to the client's interests unrelated to minimizing conviction.

Competence

Regardless of who makes the decision about waging a media campaign, the lawyer has to weigh the risks and rewards such a campaign presents. If the lawyer makes the decision, such weighing of the risks and rewards is necessary to make that decision competently. If the client makes the decision, then the lawyer needs to advise the client about that decision. Weighing the risks and rewards is just as necessary for the lawyer to act competently in the role of advisor, as it is to act competently as the decision maker.

As noted before, most criminal lawyers advise their clients not to talk to anyone, much less the media, while a case is under investigation or a charge is pending. Even high-profile defendants usually keep quiet. This suggests that lawyers and clients in most cases conclude that the risks of statements to the media typically outweigh the rewards. How does a lawyer competently decide whether the risks or rewards are greater? This is a difficult decision because it may be hard to predict how clients will present themselves, what questions might be asked, and how the public, jurors, witnesses, judges, and prosecutors will react to what the clients say. Some clients may be able to afford to hire experts to help the lawyer in making these predictions. But many will not, in which case the lawyer and client must assess the risks and rewards on their own.

With a wealthy client or a high-profile individual or corporate client, it may be a challenge for the criminal lawyer to get the client to appreciate the risks of a media campaign. Some clients—especially ones with large egos who are used to receiving positive press—may be strongly inclined to defend themselves publicly when they have been publicly attacked. A client's business advisors and business lawyers may be more concerned about reducing business damage than in minimizing the risk of conviction and may reinforce a client's inclination to speak publicly. The defense lawyer may need to work hard to get the client to understand the risks posed by public comment, most of which are not readily apparent to someone who lacks criminal trial experience.

Conflict of Interest

Which way does the lawyer's self-interest cut: in favor of or against client contact with the media? Will a lawyer's self-interest in publicity as a means to attract future business distort judgments made and advice given regarding a client's media campaign?

When clients take the unusual step of talking to the media, one must ask why they have departed from conventional wisdom. There may be legitimate reasons for both lawyer and client to engage with the media, but there is also the possibility that a lawyer with a high-profile client will offer advice that is distorted by a personal desire for publicity based on the lawyer's ego or the notion that any publicity is good for business. Conversely, a lawyer may fear that a client's media campaign will so overshadow the lawyer's role in defending the case that the lawyer is more averse to a media campaign than he or she needs to be.

Whether the lawyer advises for or against a client's possible media campaign, the advice should not be tainted by the lawyer's self-interest.

Vicarious Ethics Violations?

Model Rule 8.4(a) states that "[i]t is professional misconduct for a lawyer to: (a) violate or attempt to violate the Rules of Professional

Conduct, knowingly assist or induce another to do so, or do so *through the acts of another.*" (Emphasis added.) Comment [1] to Model Rule 8.4 provides, however, that the rule "does not prohibit a lawyer from advising a client concerning action the client is legally entitled to take." If the client is going to make statements that would violate MR 3.6 if the lawyer made them, does the lawyer violate Rule 8.4 (a) by advising, encouraging, and/or assisting the client in a public relations campaign? In other words, what if the client becomes the lawyer's mouthpiece as a way to circumvent MR 3.6?

Consider the following scenario. The defense's investigation finds damaging information about the character and credibility of a government witness. However, the lawyer concludes that he or she is barred from making a public statement about it because MR 3.6 and Comment [5] list "the character, credibility, [and] reputation . . . of a . . . witness" as subjects that are more likely than not to create prejudice. But the lawyer and client together decide to have the client hold a press conference at which the client will disclose the damaging information about the witness. Has the lawyer violated MR 3.6 through the acts of another and thus violated MR 8.4? When asked a similar question by a lawyer who was requested to assist a client in drafting an advertisement that the lawyer thought would likely materially prejudice a pending proceeding, the Massachusetts Bar ethics authority stated that "[a] lawyer who drafts an advertisement for a client to place under its own name runs a substantial risk of violation of Rules 3.6 and 8.4(a) of the Massachusetts Rules of Professional Conduct (MRPC) when the lawyer concludes that placing the same advertisement under her own name would violate Rule 3.6." (Mass. Ethics Op. 03-2 (2003).)

When a client simply passes information to the public that he or she has learned from the lawyer, such as an analysis of the weaknesses of the prosecution's case, is the client acting as the lawyer's mouthpiece if the lawyer has not assisted or suggested the disclosure? If the comment to Rule 8.4 were read broadly to permit a lawyer to provide prohibited statements to the media via the client, this strategy would allow the defense lawyer effectively to nullify MR 3.6. For that reason, it is unlikely that ethics authorities would approve of such conduct.

But do the reasons for restricting lawyer speech apply if the client is doing the talking without the lawyer's involvement? For example, isn't the lawyer more likely to have access to and mention inadmissible evidence than the client? This might be one reason for controlling lawyer assistance and involvement in client media campaigns. The lawyer's assistance may make the client's public comments as likely to damage a trial as the lawyer's comments. Imagine, for example, the lawyer passing on to the client inadmissible information such as the prior sexual history of the complaining witness in a rape case. Once in possession of this information, the client is just as capable of materially prejudicing the trial process by repeating it to the press as the client's lawyer.

At least one case has confronted this situation. In *State v. Grossberg*, 705 A.2d 608, 610 (Del. Super. Ct. 1997), the Superior Court of Delaware entered a gag order restricting the prosecutors, defense lawyers, and all law enforcement officers and other persons assisting or associated with counsel from making public comments about two capital murder cases involving the death of an infant. Statements made in accordance with Rule 3.6 of the Delaware ethics rules were exempted. Subsequent to the gag order, one of the defense lawyers arranged for his client and her parents to be interviewed by Barbara Walters for an ABC News *20/20* broadcast. During the interview, the defense lawyer directed his client to answer questions about how she felt concerning the death of her infant, her mourning the loss of her baby, and what she would say "when the Delaware prosecutors say that you are a baby-killer." The client responded to the question about being a baby-killer, "It's the furthest thing from the truth. The furthest thing. I wouldn't hurt anybody or anything, especially something of mine." (*Id.* at 611–12.) The court held that the lawyer's preparation of his client and her parents "should have been limited to those areas [on] which he himself would have been permitted to comment. Otherwise, Rule 3.6 is meaningless." (*Id.* at 613.) Because of the lawyer's attempt to circumvent Rule 3.6 through his client, and the lawyer's own statements to the media relating to the character of his client, the court revoked the lawyer's *pro hac vice* admission and removed him from the case. (*Id.*)

An ethics opinion from Pennsylvania also states that Rule 8.4 strictly limits a lawyer's preparation of a client for media interviews to areas about which the lawyer would be permitted to comment pursuant to Rule 3.6. (*See* Pennsylvania Bar Assoc. Committee on Legal Ethics and Prof'l Resp., No. 94-27 (1994).) The ethics opinion notes, however, that Rule 3.6 does not apply to the client and "the only restriction on the client's comments are those which stem from the client's own conscience." (*Id.*)

Conclusion

There are a number of ethical and strategic issues lawyers need to think through when a client is considering a media campaign. The answers to these questions are often unclear, and there is meager authority defining the ethical limits of lawyer participation in client media campaigns. Ethics committees need to address this area in greater detail to provide lawyers with more guidance. In the meantime, lawyers should be wary of becoming so enmeshed with a client media campaign as to expose themselves to charges that they used the campaign as a proxy to violate the ethical limits on lawyers' comments.

Resources for Chapter 8

Rules and Standards

Model Rules of Professional Conduct 1.2, 3.6, and 8.4(a).

Cases and Ethics Opinions

State v. Grossberg, 705 A.2d 608 (Del. Super. Ct. 1997).

Pennsylvania Bar Assoc. Committee on Legal Ethics and Prof'l Resp., No. 94-27 (1994).

Mass. Ethics Op. 03-2 (2003).

PART 4

Client Autonomy

CHAPTER 9

Client Autonomy and Choice of Counsel

Should a trial judge have the power to veto a defendant's choice of counsel in a criminal case? If so, why and under what circumstances?

The courts have long recognized that a criminal defendant's Sixth Amendment rights encompass the right to be represented by a lawyer selected by the defendant. Due to lack of financial resources, however, the universe of criminal defendants for whom choice of counsel is a meaningful right is rather small. Public defenders and other appointed counsel represent approximately 80 percent of criminal defendants, and it is well established that "a defendant may not insist on representation by an attorney he cannot afford." (*Wheat v. United States*, 486 U.S. 153, 159 (1988).) But when a criminal defendant has the means to retain counsel, judges do not typically interfere with a criminal defendant's selection of counsel.

In two particular situations, though, a trial judge does have the power to veto a defendant's choice of retained counsel. One is when the chosen lawyer is not regularly admitted to practice before the court in which the defendant is charged and moves for admission *pro hac vice*. Another is when a lawyer's representation of a criminal defendant raises an issue of conflict of interest.

We begin with a brief description of these two instances in which a judge may exercise veto power over a defendant's choice of counsel. Next we review and analyze the arguments for and against giving a judge veto power over a criminal defendant's choice of counsel.

Pro Hac Vice *Admission*

The Supreme Court addressed the issue of whether a trial judge may veto a defendant's choice of counsel in the context of *pro hac vice* admission in *U.S. v. Gonzalez-Lopez*, 548 U.S. 140 (2006). A federal trial judge in the Eastern District of Missouri had refused to admit *pro hac vice* a California lawyer the defendant had chosen as counsel. Shortly before trial, the district court explained that it had denied the lawyer *pro hac vice* admission because the court believed that the lawyer had violated Missouri's anticontact rule by communicating with a defendant in an earlier unrelated case without the permission of the lawyer then representing the defendant.

On appeal, the Eighth Circuit reversed the conviction and found that the district court had misinterpreted Missouri's anticontact rule. Because the lawyer who had been denied *pro hac vice* admission was not representing another client when the lawyer communicated with the defendant in the earlier case, the anticontact rule had not been violated. The government conceded the district court's error in denying Gonzalez-Lopez his choice of counsel. The issue before the Supreme Court was one of remedy—whether reversal and a new trial require a showing of prejudice by the defendant, an issue on which lower courts had divided. In a 5–4 decision, the Court affirmed the Eighth Circuit's reversal of conviction reasoning that the denial of the right to counsel of choice is a "structural defect" that does not require a showing of prejudice for a new trial.

Federal circuits that have addressed the standard for *pro hac vice* admission recognize that a trial judge must have good cause in order to deny *pro hac vice* admission. In *Leis v. Flynt*, 439 U.S. 438, 444–45 (1979), the Supreme Court held that lawyers have no cognizable property interest or right to appear *pro hac vice*. Accordingly, the circuits usually rely on the defendant's Sixth Amendment right to counsel as the basis for requiring a showing of good cause to deny *pro hac vice* admission.

Views about what constitutes good cause vary widely in the circuits. In the Fourth Circuit, a finding of past "unlawyerlike conduct" is sufficient. (*Thomas v. Cassidy*, 249 F.2d 91, 91 (4th Cir. 1957), *cert. denied*.) In the Fifth Circuit, the trial judge must find conduct "justifying disbarment" in order to deny a motion to appear *pro hac vice*. (*In re Evans*, 524 F.2d 1004, 1008 (5th Cir. 1975).) In the Eighth Circuit, sufficient reasons for denying *pro hac vice* admission have included use of a *pro hac vice* motion to postpone a trial and past unethical behavior. (*U.S. v. Gonzalez-Lopez*, 399 F.3d

924, 929 (8th Cir. 2005).) Additional restrictions on *pro hac vice* admission, such as requiring the association of local counsel and limiting the number of *pro hac vice* appearances per year, have been upheld.

Defense Counsel Conflicts

If a lawyer jointly represents codefendants in a federal criminal case, Federal Rule of Criminal Procedure 44(c) states that the court must "inquire about the propriety of joint representation" and "take appropriate measures to protect each defendant's right to counsel" unless the court has "good cause to believe that no conflict of interest is likely to arise." Appropriate measures may include disqualification of counsel chosen by the defendant. Many states have a similar rule of criminal procedure.

In addition to such criminal procedure rules, case law interpreting and applying the Sixth Amendment requires a judge to inquire when a possible conflict of interest on the part of defense counsel is raised with the court either by the prosecutor or the defense lawyer, even if the defendant wants to retain the lawyer despite the conflict. (*See, e.g., In re Gopman*, 531 F.2d 262, 268 (5th Cir. 1976) (affirming disqualification of defense counsel over the objection of the defendant); *United States v. Carrigan*, 543 F.2d 1053, 1058 (2d Cir. 1976) ("[T]here will be cases where the court should require separate counsel to represent certain defendants despite the expressed wishes of such defendants.") (concurring opinion).) When the judge determines that there is a nonconsentable conflict of interest, the judge must disqualify defense counsel no matter what the defendant desires in order to protect the defendant's Sixth Amendment right to adequate representation of counsel.

The Pros and Cons

As the previous discussion demonstrates, the right to choice of counsel is subject to judicial veto under some circumstances. Is it wise criminal justice policy to give judges such power? In this chapter, we review the advantages and disadvantages of giving the judge a measure of veto power over a defendant's choice of counsel in a criminal case. We start with the advantages.

One possible rationale for granting a judge veto power is paternalism. Counsel may play a critical role in determining the outcome of a criminal case, and the client might make a poor choice for a number of reasons. The client may lack both experience and expertise with criminal lawyers and the criminal justice system. The general ban on in-person client solicitation reflects the bar's fear that a lawyer may misrepresent his or her experience, qualifications, and expertise or provide a misleadingly optimistic assessment of the case as a way to gain new business. Potential clients are often in a poor position to evaluate such claims. Once chosen, a criminal lawyer exercises great and often unmonitored power to make decisions and otherwise act on behalf of the client. A trial judge, by contrast, does have experience and expertise regarding lawyers and the criminal justice system. Therefore, granting trial judges some veto power might help improve the quality of the selection of counsel and protect a defendant from a poor choice of counsel.

If a lawyer fails to provide a criminal defendant with adequate representation, proving that inadequacy and obtaining a remedy such as a new trial are quite difficult. Proving impaired representation is challenging because many decisions made by defense counsel, such as the decision to call a particular witness or raise a particular defense, are based both on judgments courts are loathe to second-guess and on factual information to which the court may not have access. Even if a defendant can demonstrate impaired representation, obtaining a new trial is difficult because of the requirement that the defendant show prejudice. Such difficulties in proving and remedying poor representation after the fact provide further reasons to protect a client from making a poor choice of counsel at the outset of the case.

Allowing judges veto power over choice of counsel might also be defended on nonpaternalistic grounds. A number of systemic reasons can be advanced in favor of allowing judges to remove lawyers they think will not adequately represent defendants. Good representation is essential for the criminal justice's adversary system to work in terms of both truth finding and law enforcement. Good representation also reduces the inefficiency of appeals, collateral review, and new trials based either on incompetence of counsel or conflict of interest. Judicial veto power may also provide a check on defendants seeking to game the criminal justice system by consciously creating grounds for appeal and collateral review based on conflict of interest and incompetent representation.

What, though, are the disadvantages of giving trial judges veto power? Choice of counsel in some cases may be the most important decision the defendant makes. The division of authority between client and attorney vests final authority in making strategic "means" decisions with the lawyer. Because the defendant has to live with the results of such decisions by counsel, it may be argued that the defendant should be given an unfettered right to choose counsel on the basis of a right to personal autonomy, the idea that people deserve to make decisions that seriously affect their lives. Such an emphasis on personal autonomy is consistent with the Court's decision in *Faretta v. California*, 422 U.S. 806, 819–20 (1977), which recognized that the defendant has the right, with some limitations, to proceed pro se as part of the defendant's Sixth Amendment right "to make his defense."

In response to the paternalism arguments advanced above, one can argue that improper motivations might distort a judge's judgment so that a veto of chosen counsel reflects the judge's own interests rather than those of the defendant. A judge's decision to deny a defendant's choice of particular counsel might improperly be influenced by bias or other perverse incentives. Bias may result from past experience with a particular lawyer or views the judge has formed about the defendant or the charged crime. A plausible perverse incentive would be the desire to increase the chances of a guilty plea to conserve judicial resources and prevent docket backlogs. Such a desire might prompt a judge to veto a lawyer who is prone to challenging the prosecution's case aggressively and not prone to disposing of cases quickly and efficiently through a guilty plea. The judge may also have an improper bias in favor of defense lawyers who have ongoing relationships with the judge and prosecutor. Indeed, a defendant may intentionally seek a defense lawyer who is not familiar with the prosecutor or judge, believing such a lawyer is insulated from the need to make concessions to the judge and prosecutor for the sake of future cases the lawyer may have with that judge and prosecutor.

From a systemic perspective, unfettered choice of counsel may also be seen as facilitating effective and efficient representation. A defendant who chooses counsel may place greater trust in that lawyer. As a result, defense counsel may more easily facilitate the full and frank discussions necessary for good legal representation and protection of the defendant's rights. Client confidence also prompts a defendant to give credence to counsel's advice and assessment of possible defenses and the reasonableness of potential plea offers by the prosecution.

A defendant who has counsel of choice is also more likely to feel better about the justice system and to accept the results that system produces. Data suggest that the incidence of ineffective assistance of counsel claims is less frequent when the client has chosen counsel. Thus, the justice system may benefit if the defendant has counsel of choice by minimizing ineffective assistance of counsel claims on appeal and in collateral review.

Conclusion

There are persuasive arguments both for and against granting judges veto power over choice of defense counsel. As often happens in such situations, the law reaches a compromise position on judicial veto power over a defendant's choice of counsel. In most instances, the law respects and defers to client choice. In our view, this deference reflects the high value we place on autonomy in the United States. Guaranteeing the right to choose counsel validates the autonomy of the individual at a time when the person's property, liberty, and life may be at stake. But, at the same time, the law recognizes a fairly narrowly circumscribed judicial veto power in situations in which systemic interests are seen as outweighing the value of autonomy.

Resources for Chapter 9

Rules and Standards

MODEL RULE OF PROFESSIONAL CONDUCT 4.2.
FEDERAL RULE OF CRIMINAL PROCEDURE 44(c).

Cases and Ethics Opinions

Thomas v. Cassidy, 249 F.2d 91 (4th Cir. 1957).
In re Evans, 524 F.2d 1004 (5th Cir. 1975).
In re Gopman, 531 F.2d 262 (5th Cir. 1976).
United States v. Carrigan, 543 F.2d 1053 (2d Cir. 1976).
Faretta v. California, 422 U.S. 806 (1977).
Leis v. Flynt, 439 U.S. 438 (1979).
Wheat v. United States, 486 U.S. 153 (1988).
U.S. v. Gonzalez-Lopez, 399 F.3d 924 (8th Cir. 2005).
U.S. v. Gonzalez-Lopez, 548 U.S. 140 (2006).

Articles, Reports, Books, and Other Sources

Janet C. Hoeffel, *Toward a More Robust Right to Counsel of Choice*, 44 SAN DIEGO L. REV. 525 (2007).

CHAPTER 10

Counsel or Client: Who's in Charge?

Which decisions in a criminal case does the client get to make? Which does defense counsel make? Although bright lines exist for who calls the shots regarding certain decisions, there are situations in which the division of authority between client and defense counsel is less than clear. In this chapter we examine the division of authority between client and attorney in a variety of contexts.

We begin with a discussion of the classic lodestars in this area: ends and means. The client determines the objectives, or ends, of the representation, whereas counsel has authority to decide the means used to achieve those goals. Next, we examine how the ethics rules and courts seek to resolve disputes between the client and defense counsel over the means of representation. In the final section of this chapter, we discuss some opinions in which courts have found that the client's silence or acquiescence in response to counsel's actions or advice constitutes a waiver of the right to make a decision. The division of authority between client and counsel can be quite nuanced, and defense counsel needs to tread carefully to meet ethical and legal obligations to clients.

Allocation of Authority

Rule 1.2 of the Model Rules of Professional Conduct provides that the client makes decisions concerning the objectives of representation. In a criminal case, the objective of representation may be avoiding conviction, pleading guilty to a lesser offense, receiving probation instead of incarceration, or receiving the lowest possible prison sentence. Model Rule 1.2 specifically provides that in criminal cases "the lawyer shall abide by a client's decision, after consultation with the lawyer, as to a plea to be entered, whether to waive jury trial and whether the client will testify." Although the client's decision of what plea to enter easily qualifies as an objective, decisions concerning whether to proceed to trial by jury or to testify expand client decisions beyond the objectives of representation to include decisions over what appear to be strategy or means of representation. Comment [2] to Rule 1.2 extends client decision making further by stating that counsel "usually defer" to the client over questions of expense or concerns for third persons, such as may be presented by a hard cross-examination of a witness.

This ethics rule's allocation of authority to the client is consistent with the Supreme Court's view in *Jones v. Barnes*, 463 U.S. 745, 751 (1983). In *Jones* the Supreme Court stated that whether to plead guilty, waive a jury, testify, or appeal are "fundamental decisions" under the Sixth Amendment that "the accused has the ultimate authority to make." In addition, the Court has recognized that, with some limitations, the defendant has the right to decide to proceed pro se, *Faretta v. California*, 422 U.S. 806 (1977), and to choice of counsel, *U.S. v. Gonzalez-Lopez*, 548 U.S. 140 (2006).

Authority to make decisions regarding the means for achieving the client's goals generally rests with defense counsel. A comment to the rule explains that the client normally defers to the lawyer to make decisions concerning "technical, legal and tactical matters" to accomplish client objectives. (Rule 1.2, cmt. [2].) Indeed, "the more technical the legal rule, the less appropriate it is for the accused to make the choice personally." (*United States v. Boyd*, 86 F.3d 719, 724 (7th Cir. 1996) (holding that decisions about which jurors to challenge are tactical ones that the lawyer makes).) Model Rule 1.2 also provides that the lawyer shall consult with the client about the means used to pursue the client's objectives.

The ABA Standards for Criminal Justice similarly provide that defense counsel has authority to make strategic and tactical decisions, after consultation with the client. Those decisions include "what witnesses to call, whether and how to conduct cross-examination, what jurors to accept or strike, what trial motions should be made, and what evidence should be introduced." (ABA CRIMINAL JUSTICE STANDARDS, DEFENSE FUNCTION, Standard 4-5.2.)

Both the Model Rule and the Criminal Justice Standards adopt a view of defense counsel expressed by former Chief Justice Warren Burger that once the defendant hires counsel or receives appointed counsel, "the day-to-day conduct of the defense rests with the attorney." (*Wainwright v. Sykes*, 433 U.S. 72, 93 (1977) (Burger,

C. J., concurring).) Burger further stated that decisions about what witnesses to call, defenses to develop, and other aspects of representation are not only decisions that "rest with the attorney" but "must as a practical matter, be made without consulting the client." (*Id.*) Both the Model Rule and the Criminal Justice Standards appear to reject Burger's "go it alone" view of lawyers in deciding tactics and require counsel to consult with the client in framing the means of representation. In practice, defense lawyers simply cannot consult with clients about all tactical decisions. The 2002 amendments to Model Rule 1.2(a) recognized this reality by adding that "[a] lawyer may take such action on behalf of a client as is impliedly authorized to carry out the representation." The legislative history of this amendment states that the "impliedly authorized" language was added to avoid the conclusion that the lawyer has to consult with the client over every matter in order to act on the client's behalf.

Courts have found that decisions concerning case scheduling, whether to file a suppression or other pretrial motion, to stipulate to easily provable facts, to strike a prospective juror, and whether to request a mistrial are strategic decisions for counsel to make.

In the following section, we look at how the ethics rules and courts seek to resolve disputes between the client and defense counsel over the means of representation.

Disputes over Means

The ethics rules do not provide clear guidance on how disputes between the client and attorney should be resolved. The comment to Model Rule 1.2 encourages the attorney to resolve disputes over means through discussion with the client, which we believe recognizes that most often the attorney will be able to persuade the client to agree to the planned strategy. The comment also states that the ethics rules do not provide how fundamental disputes over means should be resolved if there is an impasse, but that lawyer withdrawal from representation or the client discharging the lawyer are options under Model Rule 1.16. The comment additionally notes that some disputes may be resolved by "other law," which refers to cases defining the client's Sixth Amendment rights to make fundamental decisions concerning the case.

A high-profile case illustrating the difficulty in resolving a fundamental conflict between the client and defense counsel over the means of representation is the Unabomber case, *United States v. Kaczynski*, 239 F.3d 1108 (9th Cir. 2000). Ted Kaczynski's lawyers believed Kaczynski suffered from mental disease and that they were ethically compelled to present evidence of this to the court in an effort to avoid the death penalty. Kaczynski rejected this strategy, maintaining that he was sane, and he raised the conflict with the trial court. Kaczynski and his lawyers initially resolved this dispute by agreeing not to assert the insanity defense during the guilt phase of the trial but to present evidence of mental illness during the penalty phase.

After the jury was impaneled, Kaczynski made a motion to proceed pro se in order to avoid his counsel raising the mental illness issue at any part of the trial. The trial court ruled that his request to proceed pro se was too late and that it was made for tactical reasons, such as delay. After the denial of his motion to proceed pro se, Kaczynski entered a guilty plea and received consecutive life sentences, avoiding both a continued dispute over the mental illness issue and the death penalty.

Kaczynski later appealed claiming that his guilty plea was involuntary and that he had the right to prevent his lawyers from presenting the mental illness defense at any stage of the trial. The government relied on *United States v. Wadsworth*, 830 F.2d 1500, 1509 (9th Cir. 1987), for the proposition that "counsel, and not his client, is in charge of the choice of trial tactics and theory of defense" and argued that Kaczynski's lawyers had the authority to present the mental illness defense over their client's objections. The Ninth Circuit Court of Appeals affirmed the trial court's decision that the guilty plea was voluntary and did not reach the issue of who ultimately controlled the right to assert a mental defense short of an insanity defense. (*Id.* at 1118.)

The Unabomber case did not resolve the legal issue of who has authority to decide whether mental illness should be raised. But the defendant's Sixth Amendment right "to make his defense," recognized in *Faretta v. California*, 422 U.S. at 819–20, has been used by some courts as grounds for concluding that the client's right to decide the objectives of representation includes the defenses to be raised and whether mitigation evidence should be introduced.

For example, in *State v. Hedges*, 8 P.3d 1259, 1273–74 (Kan. 2000), the Kansas Supreme Court decided that a defendant competent to stand trial has the right to determine whether to assert an insanity defense. The California Supreme Court relied on *Faretta* in holding that a capital defendant has the right to offer a diminished capacity defense at the guilt or penalty phase, even if defense counsel disagrees with this defense for strategic reasons. (*People v. Frierson*, 705 P.2d 396, 403–04 (Cal. 1983).) In another capital case, *Pruitt v.*

State, 514 S.E.2d 639, 650 (Ga. 1999), the Georgia Supreme Court ruled that the defendant, not defense counsel, has the ultimate authority to decide whether to present mitigation evidence.

These cases reflect a more expansive view of client decision-making authority than the traditional objectives/means dichotomy suggests, and defense counsel should be aware that in criminal cases the allocation of decision-making authority is less clear than the ethics rule suggests. These cases also demonstrate that avoiding impasses with clients over what the lawyer views as a tactic or strategy is important. The lawyer should take the time to explain and educate the client about strategic choices. If the lawyer can convince the client that a particular strategy should be pursued, there is no need to confront the issue of who makes the decision.

Acquiescing to Counsel's Decisions

Even when a client has the right to make a decision, such as to testify or to admit guilt, silence or acquiescence in response to counsel's advice or actions can constitute a waiver of that right.

In *Frey v. Schuetzle*, 151 F.3d 893 (8th Cir. 1998), the state charged Jeffrey Frey with murder and attempted murder stemming from shootings that occurred while Frey and nine other men, including the two victims, were hunting. The night before the shootings, Frey and the others drank heavily and some used drugs. The day of the shootings, Frey and one of the other hunters were situated away from the others when Frey shot and killed the other hunter with him. Frey then shot at an abandoned building and his own pickup truck, and two pellets from Frey's shotgun ricocheted and hit a second victim standing too far away to see who fired the shotgun.

Frey initially signed a sworn statement denying any knowledge of the shootings and told his retained defense counsel that he could not remember what happened that day. The state had a strong circumstantial evidence case, and defense counsel told Frey that the only available defense was self-defense. As the trial neared, Frey told his attorney that the shooting had been in self-defense.

Frey's attorney presented a self-defense theory of the case, but Frey did not testify. Instead, the defense argued that the evidence was more consistent with self-defense than with murder and attempted murder and that the prosecution had not proven its case beyond a reasonable doubt. Frey was convicted.

In a habeas corpus action, Frey argued that he did not knowingly and voluntarily waive his right to testify in his own behalf.

Frey claimed that he told his attorney that he wanted to testify, and that his counsel told Frey that he should not. Frey further claimed that he believed that his attorney had the authority to decide whether Frey would testify. Frey's attorney stated that he had informed Frey of his right to testify and that Frey agreed with his advice not to testify. The transcript of the trial demonstrated that Frey was present when the judge stated that Frey had the right to testify if he chose, and that Frey did not object when his counsel rested his case without calling Frey to the stand.

The district court concluded that Frey knowingly and voluntarily waived his right to testify, relying in large part on Frey's failure to object to not being called as a witness. On appeal, the Eight Circuit affirmed.

A case involving both a client's acquiescence and the blurring of the line between a client's fundamental decision over objectives and a defense lawyer's strategy is *Florida v. Nixon*, 543 U.S. 175 (2004). In *Nixon*, the Supreme Court examined whether defense counsel could concede guilt in the trial phase of a capital case in order to "preserve his [counsel's] credibility" for presenting extensive mitigation evidence of the defendant's mental instability during the penalty phase.

In *Nixon*, the defendant confessed to a brutal kidnapping and killing. The state indicted Nixon for first-degree murder, a capital offense in Florida, and Nixon's public defender investigated the case, including deposing all of the prosecution's witnesses. Defense counsel attempted to plea bargain the matter, but the prosecutor refused to recommend any sentence less than death. Faced with going to trial on the capital charge, counsel concluded that the best strategy would be to concede guilt and then present extensive mitigation evidence during the penalty phase.

Counsel met with Nixon several times to explain the strategy, but Nixon was unresponsive and never verbally approved or rejected the strategy. At trial, Nixon became very disruptive and was absent during much of the trial. In opening statement during the guilt phase of the trial, counsel acknowledged Nixon's guilt and urged the jury to focus on the penalty phase. During the trial, counsel fully participated, contesting the introduction of some evidence as prejudicial, and cross-examining the state's witnesses. In closing argument, counsel again acknowledged Nixon's guilt. During the penalty phase, counsel argued "that Nixon was not 'an intact human being' and that he had committed the murder while afflicted with multiple mental disabilities." (*Id.* at 183–84.)

After deliberating for three hours, the jury recommended the death sentence and the judge imposed it. On appeal, new counsel argued that the concession of guilt by defense counsel was the functional equivalent of a guilty plea that required Nixon's express consent. Appellate counsel argued that *Boykin v. Alabama*, 395 U.S. 238, 242–43 (1969), required that a guilty plea be based on express, voluntary affirmations and could not be inferred from silence. The Florida Supreme Court agreed and reversed the conviction holding that without the defendant's express consent, a concession of guilt was prejudicial ineffective assistance of counsel requiring a new trial.

The Supreme Court reversed, stating that the defense counsel's concession of guilt was not equivalent to a guilty plea in a two-stage capital trial. The Court reasoned that when counsel informs the defendant of a strategy that counsel believes to be in the client's best interests and the client is unresponsive, "counsel's strategic choice . . . [should] not [be] impeded by any blanket rule demanding defendant's explicit consent." (543 U.S. at 192.) Instead, the Court held that such strategic decisions should be analyzed subject to *Strickland v. Washington*, 466 U.S. 668 (1984), which requires a defendant to demonstrate both deficient performance by counsel that falls below "an objective standard of reasonableness" and prejudice that "deprive[s] the defendant of a fair trial, a trial whose result is reliable." (*Id*. at 687–68.)

The Court's decision in *Nixon* exemplifies two judicial trends. First, as the Eighth Circuit did in *Frey*, courts tend to interpret a defendant's silence after consultation with defense counsel as acquiescence to defense counsel's advice or action even when the action may waive a defendant's fundamental right. Second, courts give great deference to the strong presumption announced in *Strickland* that defense counsel's conduct "'might be considered sound trial strategy'" and courts should be "highly deferential." (466 U.S. at 689.)

Conclusion

Division of authority between the client and attorney in criminal cases is not simply an ends/means analysis. The ethics rules explicitly recognize that clients in criminal cases will decide much more than the plea to enter by extending client decisions to the arguably strategic issues of whether to waive a jury or to testify, and by requiring counsel to consult with the client over other means to achieve the client's objectives. A client's Sixth Amendment right to make a defense has been used by courts to extend client decision making further into areas that could be considered the means of representation, such as raising a mental incapacity defense or presenting mitigation evidence. At the same time, courts have also found that the client can waive the right to decide by remaining silent or failing to object to a particular course of action at trial. Finally, courts often defer to counsel decisions, and there is strong presumption that many of the day-to-day decisions are strategic ones that counsel has the authority to make.

Resources for Chapter 10

Rules and Standards

MODEL RULES OF PROFESSIONAL CONDUCT 1.2 and 1.16.

ABA CRIMINAL JUSTICE STANDARDS FOR THE DEFENSE FUNCTION, Standard 4-5.2.

Cases and Ethics Opinions

Boykin v. Alabama, 395 U.S. 238 (1969).
Faretta v. California, 422 U.S. 806 (1977).
Wainwright v. Sykes, 433 U.S. 72 (1977).
Jones v. Barnes, 463 U.S. 745 (1983).
People v. Frierson, 705 P.2d 396 (Cal. 1983).
Strickland v. Washington, 466 U.S. 668 (1984).
United States v. Wadsworth, 830 F.2d 1500 (9th Cir. 1987).
United States v. Boyd, 86 F.3d 719 (7th Cir. 1996).
Frey v. Schuetzle, 151 F.3d 893 (8th Cir. 1998).
Pruitt v. State, 514 S.E.2d 639 (Ga. 1999).
United States v. Kaczynski, 239 F.3d 1108 (9th Cir. 2000).
State v. Hedges, 8 P.3d 1259 (Kan. 2000).
Florida v. Nixon, 543 U.S. 175 (2004).
U.S. v. Gonzalez-Lopez, 548 U.S. 140 (2006).

Articles, Reports, Books, and Other Sources

Kimberly Helene Zelnick, *In Gideon's Shadow: The Loss of Defendant Autonomy and the Growing Scope of Attorney Discretion*, 30 AM. J. CRIM. L. 363 (2003).

Robert E. Toone, *The Incoherence of Defendant Autonomy*, 83 N.C.L. REV. 621 (2005).

PART 5

Conflicts of Interest

CHAPTER 11

The Supreme Court and Defense Counsel Conflicts

Conflict of interest issues arise in criminal cases in many contexts. A single lawyer or different lawyers in the same firm may represent two or more codefendants. A lawyer may represent a defendant in a case as well as the alleged victim or a key prosecution witness. Or a lawyer may represent a defendant in a case in which a former client is the alleged victim or a key prosecution witness. In each instance, obligations to a current or former client pose a risk of impairing the lawyer's representation of a client. If convicted, the client is likely to challenge the lawyer's performance as constitutionally ineffective. In this chapter, we examine the Supreme Court's approach to conflict of interest and criminal defense counsel.

The Legal Standard

Ineffective assistance claims typically require that the claimant show two elements: first, objectively unreasonable performance by the lawyer, and second, prejudice—a reasonable probability that the lawyer's inadequate performance adversely affected the outcome of the case. (*See Strickland v. Washington*, 466 U.S. 668, 687 (1984).) The Court has not applied the *Strickland* test, however, to ineffective assistance claims based on conflict of interest. In the conflicts area, the Court has used a number of different tests. In some situations, the claimant must show not only an actual conflict but one that adversely affected the lawyer's performance. (*See Cuyler v. Sullivan*, 446 U.S. 335, 348 (1980).) In other situations, the

Court has appeared to dispense with the adverse impact element, and require only an actual conflict. (*See Wood v. Georgia*, 450 U.S. 261, 272 (1981) (holding that when "the possibility of a conflict of interest" is "sufficiently apparent . . . the court [has] a duty to inquire further").) In still other situations, automatic reversal is warranted without a showing of either an actual conflict or adverse impact on the defense lawyer's performance. (*See Holloway v. Arkansas*, 435 U.S. 475, 488–89 (1978).)

Which of these tests should apply to a situation in which, first, the trial judge knew or should have known about a conflict but failed to conduct an inquiry, and second, the claimant was never informed of the conflict? That was the key issue in *Mickens v. Taylor*, 535 U.S. 162 (2002).

Mickens v. Taylor: *The Facts*

On March 20, 1992, Bryan Saunders was appointed to represent Timothy Hall, a 17-year-old charged with assaulting his mother and possessing a concealed weapon. Saunders subsequently met with Hall to discuss the charges. Saunders, though, never had to appear in court because Hall was killed before his case was resolved. On April 3, 1992, Judge Aundria Foster dismissed the charges against Hall.

The next day, police arrested Walter Mickens for the murder and attempted forcible sodomy of Hall. On April 6, Judge Foster telephoned Saunders and asked him to accept an appointment to represent Mickens. Saunders accepted, never mentioning his prior representation of Hall to the trial court, cocounsel, or Mickens. Convicted and sentenced in state court to death, Mickens filed a federal habeas petition in which his new counsel for the first time discovered Saunders's prior representation of Hall. In his federal habeas case, Mickens raised a Sixth Amendment ineffective assistance of counsel argument based on conflict of interest due to Saunders's undisclosed prior representation of Hall.

The Conflict in Mickens

Was there a substantial risk that Saunders's prior representation of Hall would impair his representation of Mickens? Once a representation is concluded, a lawyer typically no longer advises or acts on behalf of a former client, especially a deceased one. Ethics doctrine on conflicts between past and present clients tends to focus on issues of confidentiality, because the obligations of confidentiality continue to bind the lawyer even after a representation has ended. In the typical case, the concern is that the former client will be hurt by the current client having access to the former client's confidences.

The district court in Mickens's habeas case found that Saunders met with Hall and that there were at least four confidences from Hall that were relevant to Mickens's case and that Saunders was prohibited from revealing under the Virginia Code of Professional Responsibility DR 4-101: (1) Hall had been charged with carrying a concealed weapon; (2) Hall's mother had pressed charges against him for assault; (3) Hall was not living with his mother at the time of his death; and (4) Saunders had discussed with Hall "the circumstances surrounding each of the charged crimes." (*Mickens v. Greene*, 74 F. Supp. 2d 586, 599–600 (E.D. Va. 1999).)

How, though, could Mickens be hurt in this situation when Hall's confidences were at risk and Mickens could have benefited from such a disclosure? The concern here is that Saunders's obligations to Hall created incentives for Saunders to avoid investigating Hall. As the Court recognized in *Holloway*, "representation of conflicting interests is suspect because of what it tends to prevent the attorney from doing." (*Holloway*, 435 U.S. at 489.) As Mickens's lawyer, Saunders was obligated to investigate "all avenues leading to facts relevant to the merits of the case and the penalty in the event of conviction." (ABA Standards of Criminal Justice § 4-4-1(a) (1991).) This duty included investigating potentially embarrassing behavior by Hall, including the criminal conduct of Hall during the time Hall was Saunders's client. At odds with this duty to investigate was Saunders's duty to maintain confidentiality regarding the information concerning Hall's criminal charges, his strained family relationship, and any other information Hall may have disclosed to Saunders that might have helped Mickens. "The mere presence of an attorney does not fulfill the Sixth Amendment guarantee when the advocate's conflicting obligations have effectively sealed his lips on crucial matters." (*Holloway*, 435 U.S. at 490.)

The "substantial relationship" test is the classic standard for assessing successive conflict of interest between a present client and a former client—the sort of conflict that existed in the *Mickens* case. That test states that a lawyer "may not . . . represent another client in the same or a substantially related matter in which the interests of the former client are materially adverse" unless "both the affected present and former clients consent to the representation." (RESTATEMENT OF THE LAW GOVERNING LAWYERS § 132 (2000).)

Because Saunders could have obtained from Hall information that would prove relevant in Mickens's case, the cases were substantially related. (*See Analytica, Inc. v. NPD Research, Inc.*, 708 F.2d 1263 (7th Cir. 1983).) And the interests of Hall and Mickens, as crime victim and defendant, were obviously adverse to one another. Accordingly, ethics doctrine views Saunders as having had a conflict of interest.

The Court's Decision in Mickens

Prior to Mickens's case reaching the Supreme Court, some lower courts had applied *Holloway*'s automatic reversal rule even when defense counsel failed to advise the trial court of the possible conflict. (See, e.g., *Armienti v. United States*, 234 F.3d 820 (2d Circ. 2000).) In *Mickens*, the district court and en banc Fourth Circuit held that the *Cuyler* standard applied to such a case and found that Mickens failed to show adverse impact on his lawyer's performance. Two judges on the Fourth Circuit panel, who became dissenters to the en banc opinion, concluded that a more lenient standard applied under which Mickens needed to prove only an actual conflict. The dissenters relied on *Wood v. Georgia*, 450 U.S. 261, 272 (1981), for the proposition that adverse affect is not required "when the trial court has failed to make an inquiry even though it knows or reasonably should know that a particular conflict exists." These judges found that Mickens met the *Wood* test because the trial judge "knew or should have known about an apparent conflict" and failed to conduct an inquiry. (*Mickens*, 227 F.3d at 211.)

Writing for the Supreme Court in a 5–4 decision, Justice Scalia held that *Holloway*'s automatic reversal rule did not apply, and would apply only "where the defense counsel is forced to represent codefendants over his timely objections, unless the trial court has determined that there is no conflict." (*Mickens*, 535 U.S. at 168.) Because the defense counsel in *Mickens* did not raise the conflict of interest with the trial judge, the Court held that Mickens would have "to establish that the conflict of interest adversely affected his counsel's performance." (*Id.* at 174.) Rather than using *Mickens* as an opportunity to improve its Sixth Amendment conflict of interest jurisprudence by abandoning both its use of the term *actual conflict of interest*, as well as *Cuyler*'s adverse impact requirement, the Court limited the automatic reversal rule in *Holloway* to the facts in that case.

Actual Conflict

Courts and commentators have often employed the phrase *actual conflict of interest*. At times *actual conflict* is used to refer retrospectively to a situation in which a conflict of interest has already resulted in impairment of the lawyer's representation of a client. At other times, an *actual conflict* is defined prospectively as one in which "the lawyer's independent professional judgment . . . will be adversely affected." (*See In re Porter*, 584 P.2d 744, 747 (Or. 1978).) The Supreme Court stated in *Young v. United States ex rel. Vuitton*, 481 U.S. 787 (1987) that "[a]n arrangement represents an actual conflict of interest if its potential for misconduct is deemed intolerable." Unfortunately, the Supreme Court's definition provides no criteria for determining when a conflict of interest's potential for misconduct becomes intolerable.

One remedy for this situation would be for the Court to abandon use of the phrase *actual conflict of interest* in favor of the phrase *conflict of interest* as defined by ethics authorities. The Restatement of the Law Governing Lawyers, for example, defines a conflict of interest as "a substantial risk that the lawyer's representation of the client would be materially and adversely affected by the lawyer's own interest or the lawyer's duties to another current client, a former client, or a third person." (RESTATEMENT OF THE LAW GOVERNING LAWYERS § 121 (2000).) The Model Rules now define a conflict of interest as "a significant risk that the representation of one or more clients will be materially limited by the lawyer's responsibilities to another client, a former client or a third person or by a personal interest of the lawyer." The Restatement and Model Rule definitions are preferable because they clearly state that conflict of interest is about risk of impairment, and that the acceptability of such risk is determined by its magnitude (i.e., "substantial" or "significant"). If the Supreme Court were to use the term *conflict of interest* as defined by ethics authorities, it would clarify the Court's terminology as well as its analysis of conflicts and the proper remedies.

Adverse Impact?

Sixth Amendment jurisprudence requiring defendants to demonstrate "adverse impact" poses significant proof problems for defendants. The decisions lawyers make on behalf of criminal defendants—deciding what strategies to use at trial, for example, or what evidence to present at sentencing—often require complex judgments involving many factors that cannot be measured with precision. And the processes by which lawyers resolve such questions are largely internal, almost never on the record, and not easily subject to proof by the client, especially months or even years later. Conditioning enforcement of conflicts rules on proof of adverse impact makes them hard to enforce ex post and undermines their deterrent effect ex ante.

The Supreme Court has recognized as much. In *Holloway*, the Court made clear that when a judge fails to explore the risks of a conflict raised by a defendant's objection at the trial, reversal is automatic without a showing of either adverse impact on the lawyer's performance or the outcome of the trial. The Court stated that requiring a defendant to show an adverse impact on the lawyer's performance or outcome at trial "in some specific fashion would not be susceptible of intelligent, even-handed application." (*Holloway*, 435 U.S. at 489.) It reasoned that if a conflict causes a defense lawyer to refrain from taking action, it is difficult to assess the impact of the conflict because the record is silent.

In *Mickens*, Saunders was ethically required to reveal the conflict to Mickens and the court. If Saunders had disclosed his prior representation of Hall, then Mickens could have decided whether or not to waive the conflict and the court would have been required to investigate the conflict to determine if Mickens made a fully informed, knowing waiver. The court would also have been required to determine if Saunders was laboring under a conflict so great that it could not have been waived. By failing to reveal the conflict, Saunders denied Mickens his right to consent and the court the opportunity to police the conflict and maintain the integrity of the trial process.

The facts in *Mickens* demonstrate how an adverse impact rule imposes an almost insurmountable burden of proof on a defendant. Mickens would have had to have access to the confidences Hall disclosed to Saunders to demonstrate how the conflict between Saunders's obligation to Hall and his duties to Mickens adversely impacted the representation or the outcome of his case.

In addition to addressing these pragmatic proof concerns, a risk approach engenders greater confidence on the part of the defendant and the public in the quality of defense representation, especially in a death penalty case. In short, neither Mickens nor the public should have to speculate about whether Saunders's past representation of Hall impaired his representation of Mickens.

Conclusion

The Supreme Court unfortunately failed to grasp the opportunity in *Mickens* to take significant remedial steps regarding defense counsel and conflict of interest. First, the Court should have simplified its conflict of interest terminology by abandoning the phrase *actual conflict of interest* and using, instead, just *conflict of interest* as defined by ethics authorities. Second, the Court should have changed its approach to conflicts by focusing on the risks presented by a conflict and not requiring a defendant to prove adverse impact either on the lawyer's representation or the outcome at trial or sentencing.

Resources for Chapter 11

Rules and Standards

MODEL RULES OF PROFESSIONAL CONDUCT 1.7 and 1.9.

Cases and Ethics Opinions

Holloway v. Arkansas, 435 U.S. 475, 488–89 (1978).
In re Porter, 584 P.2d 744 (Or. 1978).
Cuyler v. Sullivan, 446 U.S. 335 (1980).
Wood v. Georgia, 450 U.S. 261 (1981).
Analytica, Inc. v. NPD Research, Inc., 708 F.2d 1263 (7th Cir. 1983).
Armienti v. United States, 234 F.3d 820 (2d Circ. 2000).
Strickland v. Washington, 466 U.S. 668 (1984).
Mickens v. Taylor, 535 U.S. 162 (2002).
Young v. United States ex rel. Vuitton, 481 U.S. 787 (1987).

Articles, Reports, Books, and Other Sources

Patrice McGuire Sabach, *Rethinking Unwaivable Conflicts of Interest after* United States v. Scharz *and* Mickens v. Taylor, 59 N.Y.U. ANN. SURV. AM. L. 89 (2003).
RESTATEMENT OF THE LAW GOVERNING LAWYERS §§ 121, 132 (2000).

CHAPTER 12

Campaign Pledges to Prosecute

Should a lawyer running for election to a prosecutor's office make a campaign pledge to prosecute a particular person if elected? If elected after making such a pledge, should the prosecutor be disqualified from participation in the trial of that person?

Given the immense power vested in the prosecutor and the fact that more than 95 percent of chief prosecutors at the state and local levels are elected, it is surprising that both legal commentators and the media have largely ignored the ethics of pledges to prosecute. In this chapter, we explore this neglected intersection of politics and ethics.

An Explicit Pledge to Prosecute

A rare reported case examining an explicit campaign pledge to prosecute is *State v. Hohman*, 420 A.2d 852 (Vt. 1980). Hohman was convicted of homicide, but the conviction was reversed based on erroneous admission of evidence. Shortly after remand, the prosecutor found himself in what the Vermont Supreme Court termed "a battle for re-election." During the election, the prosecutor ran a newspaper ad in which he stated, "The *Hohman* case is the most important case pending. . . . If I am re-elected, I will vigorously prosecute Hohman and obtain a second conviction." (*Id.* at 854.)

The prosecutor was reelected, the defendant moved to disqualify him, and the trial court denied the motion. The Vermont Supreme Court found that the prosecutor's campaign pledge constituted misconduct, stating, "We strongly condemn the conduct of the state's attorney in this case. The awesome power to prosecute ought never to be manipulated for personal or political profit." (*Id.* at 855.) The court concluded that "it was error for the state's attorney to fail to disqualify himself, and it was error for the trial court to deny the motion to disqualify the state's attorney." (*Id.*) Moreover, the court referred the matter to Vermont's Professional Conduct Board.

Despite its unequivocal condemnation of the prosecutor's campaign pledge, the Vermont Supreme Court did not explain why this conduct was wrong. The court simply quoted the famous passage from *Berger v. United States,* concerning a prosecutor's obligation to see "that justice shall be done," and referred the matter to disciplinary authorities citing Vermont Code of Professional Responsibility Disciplinary Rule 7-107 about public comment during pending criminal matters.

It is not clear, though, how this sort of pledge to prosecute falls within the terms of DR 7-107. The most plausible part of DR 7-107 a campaign pledge to prosecute might arguably violate is its ban on "opinions as to the guilt or innocence of the accused, the evidence, or the merits of the case." Essentially this same language is found in Rule 3.6 Comment [5] of the ABA Model Rules of Professional Conduct. Such a pledge undoubtedly implies, though it does not directly state, an opinion about the defendant's guilt and the merits of the case. But if statements that imply such opinions violate the rules on trial publicity, then any announcement by a prosecutor of a decision to prosecute would appear to violate DR 7-107 as well as Model Rule 3.6.

What's Wrong with a Pledge to Prosecute?

The overwhelming majority of this country's chief prosecutors are elected. Shouldn't the voting public be as informed about candidates' positions on prosecuting particular defendants as it is about their positions on other criminal justice issues? By electing a prosecutor, the public exercises power over issues such as police corruption, sentencing policies, and how limited criminal justice resources should be spent. Why shouldn't public debate and power extend to which defendants a prosecutor will pursue?

Political Distortion

It can be very tempting for a candidate to make a campaign pledge to prosecute an individual. Vivid, concrete images from a specific crime, such as those in the Megan Kanka, Polly Klaus, and John

Hinkley cases, have greater psychological impact on the public's thinking than does abstract discussion of crime legislation. The power of these vivid images provides a candidate with both an opportunity and a motive to craft a pledge to prosecute an individual in order to stand out in the minds of voters. For this reason, there is substantial risk that decisions made in the heat of a political contest will be bad ones, driven by politics rather than justice. Defendants charged in the aftermath of such campaign posturing also run the risk of suffering unduly harsh treatment.

Decisions Made on Incomplete Information

Another concern is that decisions about a prosecution made prior to election are likely to be based on inadequate information and unlikely to be modified once a candidate is elected and receives more complete information. Studies show that most people are reluctant to change adopted positions, even if new information puts the initial position in question. This reluctance is reinforced if positions have been adopted publicly. This phenomenon, termed *nonrational escalation of commitment*, should be of particular concern in regard to prosecutors. Recent studies reveal early police and prosecutor commitments to prosecuting particular individuals based on incomplete information and reinforced by nonrational escalation to those commitments as factors in wrongful convictions. A campaign pledge to prosecute an individual is a classic example of an early and public commitment based on incomplete information. It creates a psychological barrier to the prosecutor acting in a way that later information may show to be both wise and fair.

A nonrational escalation of commitment appears to have been the downfall of Michael Nifong, the prosecutor in the Duke lacrosse team rape case. Nifong sought and obtained an indictment of three members of the Duke lacrosse team while running for election. During his election campaign, Nifong gave numerous interviews about the case and made a series of derogatory comments about the defendants, repeatedly stating their guilt. Nifong then failed to turn over to the defense favorable DNA evidence, and he instructed the lab director conducting DNA tests to produce an incomplete report noting only positive matches. The defense charged that Nifong used the case for political gain, and filed an ethics complaint against him. North Carolina later disbarred Nifong. Among the various bases for disbarment, North Carolina found that his extrajudicial statements violated Rule 3.6 and Rule 3.8(f) of the North Carolina Rules of Professional Conduct.

Constraining the Exercise of Prosecutorial Discretion

Rules constraining lawyer speech typically focus on impairment of the right to a fair trial. The concern is that public statements by lawyers will distort the trial process—altering the testimony of witnesses, undermining rules excluding evidence, and creating pressure on jurors to disregard their legal obligations. Though campaign pledges to prosecute may expose jurors and witnesses to information and opinions prior to trial, of greater concern is how such pledges may distort the pretrial functioning of the prosecutor.

The exercise of prosecutorial discretion is critical to the functioning of the criminal justice system. During the pretrial period, decisions are made on whether to prosecute, the selection of charges, and whether and how to negotiate a guilty plea. Because the overwhelming majority of criminal cases are resolved through some exercise of prosecutorial discretion regarding charging and plea negotiations, safeguarding the wise use of this discretionary power should be a primary concern of judges and ethics officials. The *Hohman* court acknowledged as much when it described Hohman as having been "prejudiced at the plea bargaining stage of these proceedings." (*State v. Hohman*, 420 A.2d at 855.)

An Implicit Pledge to Prosecute?

What if a prosecutor makes no explicit pledge to prosecute an individual, but conducts a campaign in a way that strongly implies such a pledge? A divided Colorado Supreme Court addressed this issue in *People v. N.R.*, 139 P.3d 671 (Co. 2006).

After a single-vehicle accident resulted in the death of a 15-year-old driver, the prosecutor declined to press charges against N.R., the 16-year-old passenger, who fled the scene without reporting the accident to police. Having investigated the case, the prosecutor determined there was not sufficient evidence to convict the youth of a crime.

Two years later, a new prosecutor, who had campaigned with substantial public support from the family of the deceased driver, was voted into office. Shortly after winning the election, the prosecutor charged N.R. with, among other crimes, attempted murder. Although no explicit pledge to prosecute was made, the circumstantial evidence indicates that the candidate implied as much to the driver's family and to the public.

At first glance, the situation in *People v. N.R.* may seem less dangerous than the situation in *Hohman*, because *N.R.* involved an implicit pledge whereas *Hohman* involved an explicit pledge. But another aspect of *N.R.* shows that in some ways the pledge in that case posed more danger than the one in *Hohman*. In *Hohman*, the prosecutor was an incumbent already intimately familiar with the case, having tried the case before the campaign pledge. In *N.R.*, the candidate was not an incumbent and, thus, would not have had access to the same level of information as a prosecutor in office. Such a candidate's access to information would be particularly limited in a case involving a juvenile because access to information in juvenile cases is tightly controlled.

Conclusion

The risks posed by campaign pledges are substantial. But how should judges and ethics officials classify them for purposes of ethics enforcement? One possibility, suggested by the *Hohman* court's citation of DR 7-107, is to treat them under the rules about public comment. For the reasons stated previously, we think this is not the best way to analyze campaign pledges. Another possibility is to apply an appearance of impropriety standard, as the trial court did in the *N.R.* case, when it disqualified the prosecutor. But reliance on an appearance of impropriety does not strike us as the proper approach either. For one thing, many jurisdictions have eliminated appearance of impropriety as a basis for an ethics violation. More importantly, classifying campaign pledges as simply appearing improper fails to acknowledge the genuine and substantial risks such pledges pose.

Conflict of interest, properly understood, is about barring lawyers from doing things that create a substantial and unjustifiable risk of fulfillment of the lawyer's ethical obligations. So defined, campaign pledges qualify as prosecutorial conflicts of interest. Some jurisdictions, though, may view conflict of interest more narrowly. In those jurisdictions, the best approach may be for judges to use their residual inherent power to regulate lawyers who practice before them to declare such pledges improper and to disqualify candidates who make them from later representing the government in a case in which the prosecutor has made such a pledge.

Resources for Chapter 12

Rules and Standards

MODEL RULE OF PROFESSIONAL CONDUCT 3.6.

VERMONT CODE OF PROFESSIONAL RESPONSIBILITY DISCIPLINARY RULE 7-107.

Cases and Ethics Opinions

State v. Hohman, 420 A.2d 852 (Vt. 1980).

People v. N.R., 139 P.3d 671 (Co. 2006).

PART 6

Investigation and Discovery

CHAPTER 13

To Tape or Not to Tape: Secret Recording

One person secretly taping a conversation with another is not uncommon. Scott Peterson's girlfriend secretly taped him. Linda Tripp covertly recorded her conversations with Monica Lewinsky. Richard Nixon apparently taped his conversations with everyone in the Oval Office. In each instance, the recordings proved to be powerful evidence, illustrating why lawyers may be tempted to secretly record conversations. But is a lawyer ethically permitted to tape conversations secretly? If so, under what circumstances?

This chapter explores the subject of secret recording by lawyers not engaged in law enforcement activities. We begin with an analysis and overview of the arguments for and against allowing secret taping. Next, we review the current state of the law and ethics of secret taping.

The Pros and Cons

The advantages and disadvantages of allowing lawyers to secretly record conversations may be assessed from the points of view of our justice system, the legal profession, the lawyer who does the recording, and the client.

From a systemic perspective, recording what a potential witness has to say helps prevent loss of evidence due to memory failure and the conscious or unconscious distortion of testimony by information learned at a later point by the witness. It may discourage or expose later testimony that is unreliable or perjured.

From the point of view of the organized bar, secret taping has both a positive and a negative aspect. If such taping results in more information to resolve factual issues and increases the reliability of witness testimony, then the bar might see it as improving our justice system. The negative aspect is that secret taping by lawyers may be seen as deceptive and reflect badly on the profession.

From the lawyer's perspective, there is a benefit in documenting exactly what is said by someone unaware that a conversation is being taped. For example, a defense lawyer talking with a witness could use a secret tape recording to help prove that the lawyer did not intimidate, coerce, or bribe the witness. Just as taping police interrogations protects police from false charges of misconduct, secretly taping witnesses can protect the lawyer from later false misconduct allegations by a witness or by the prosecution. Of course, the lawyer could openly tape interviews or have a third party present, such as an investigator, but the lawyer may believe that such arrangements would lead to witnesses being more guarded or refusing to talk.

From the client's perspective, secret taping by one's lawyer may give the client access to exculpatory information the client might not otherwise have and allow the lawyer to impeach false or unreliable testimony against the client. A potential downside for the client is that such recordings may constitute discoverable material. Under Federal Rule of Criminal Procedure 26.2 and many reciprocal state discovery rules, for example, prior recorded statements by a defense witness must be turned over to the prosecution for use in impeachment. If the recording provides a means for impeaching a witness who testifies favorably for the defense, then the recording could wind up hurting the client's position.

A fairness rationale relying on balance or symmetry between the prosecution and the defense may also be offered in support of secret taping. Because the government is allowed to use secret taping to gather evidence, if the defense is not allowed to do the same, doesn't that give the government an unfair advantage?

The Law on Secret Recording

Federal statutes and more than two-thirds of state statutes permit the taping of conversations as long as one party to the conversation consents. It is therefore legal for a lawyer in most states to secretly record a conversation with a potential witness. But it is almost always illegal for the lawyer to arrange to record a potential witness's conversation with another if at least one of the parties to the conversation has not consented. In addition, federal law provides that no part of an illegally intercepted oral or wire conversation may be admitted into evidence. (*See* 18 U.S.C. § 2515.)

When a conversation is lawfully recorded, a lawyer may seek to admit it into evidence if it is used to impeach or there is an applicable hearsay exception. A criminal defense lawyer's most likely use of a tape recording is to impeach a witness with a recorded prior inconsistent statement.

The Ethics of Secret Recording

Ethics codes, such as the ABA Model Rules of Professional Conduct, do not specifically address covert recording by lawyers. However, the secret recording of conversations potentially implicates a number of general ethical standards.

Model Rule 8.4 states that it is "professional misconduct for a lawyer to . . . engage in conduct involving dishonesty, fraud, deceit, or misrepresentation." DR 1-102(A)(4) of the Model Code of Professional Responsibility had a virtually identical prohibition. Is the secret tape recording of conversations inherently deceitful? The ABA initially thought so.

The ABA Standing Committee on Ethics and Professional Responsibility addressed secret recordings in 1974. Noting that it was not a federal crime to make secret recordings when one is a party to the conversation, the Standing Committee nonetheless relied on both Canon Nine's proscription that a lawyer "should avoid even the appearance of impropriety" and DR 1-102's prohibition against conduct involving "dishonesty, fraud, deceit, or misrepresentation" as "clearly encompass[ing] the making of recordings without the consent of all parties." (ABA Formal Op. 337 (1974).) The Standing Committee added that under "extraordinary circumstances" a prosecutor "might ethically make and use secret recordings if acting within strict statutory limitations conforming to constitutional requirements." (*Id.*)

The Standing Committee affirmed Formal Opinion 337 a year later, and stated that a lawyer was also ethically prohibited from directing an investigator to tape record a conversation without the knowledge of the other party. (ABA Informal Op. 1320 (1975).) Today, Model Rule 5.3 makes it clear that the lawyer is ethically responsible for the conduct of a nonlawyer assistant, and Model Rule 8.4 states that it is professional misconduct to violate the Rules of Professional Conduct "through the acts of another."

In the years after the ABA issued these two ethics opinions, many state ethics authorities followed them. Others did not, concluding that when done legally, a lawyer is ethically permitted to secretly record conversations.

The State Bar of Arizona Ethics Committee considered whether an investigator retained by a public defender could surreptitiously tape an interview with a potential witness "to obtain impeachment material on the witness should the testimony of the witness be different at the trial than in the interview." (Ariz. Op. 90-02 (1990).) In reversing an earlier opinion prohibiting secret recordings, the ethics committee stated, "The practicalities of the present day criminal justice system seem to be inconsistent with any continued prohibition against surreptitious recordation of a witness." (*Id.*) The committee gave several reasons for its decision. First, secret recording was legal under federal and state law in Arizona. Second, when an investigator interviews a witness, the investigator is not required to advise the witness that the investigator may later impeach the witness should the witness's story change on the stand. The ethics committee noted that a tape recording would be a much more accurate method for impeachment than just the testimony of the investigator. Third, if law enforcement agents may use secret recordings, the criminal defense attorney should also have that tool available to fulfill "legal and ethical duties to zealously represent a client." Finally, a number of other jurisdictions had ethics opinions approving of secret recording and Arizona no longer had an ethics rule prohibiting "the appearance of impropriety." (*Id.*)

The ABA Standing Committee withdrew Opinion 337 in 2001. The ABA's current position is that "[a] lawyer who electronically records a conversation without the knowledge of the other party or parties to the conversation does not necessarily violate the Model Rules." (ABA Formal Op. 01-422 (2001).) As do ethics opinions from several states, the ABA opinion advises that a lawyer may not make secret recordings in violation of the law, "nor falsely represent that a conversation is not being recorded." (*Id.*)

In reaching this new position on the ethics of secret recording, the ABA noted that its prior opinion relied on the prohibition against the appearance of impropriety, which does not appear in the Model Rules. Further, Model Rule 4.4, dealing with "respect for rights of third persons," proscribes only "means that have no substantial purpose other than to embarrass, delay or burden a third person," and "methods of obtaining evidence that violate the legal rights of such a person." By implication, the ABA sees conduct that has a valid purpose and does not violate a person's legal rights as permitted by Model Rule 4.4. Thus, prior Opinion 337 was at odds with the Model Rules. The ABA's new position on secret recording is consistent with a growing number of state ethics opinions.

In specifically advising against making a false denial that a conversation is being taped, the ABA Standing Committee noted that such a statement would likely violate Model Rule 4.1's prohibition against making a false statement of material fact to a third person. This same conclusion was reached in a pair of Mississippi disciplinary cases. (*See Attorney M. v. Mississippi*, 621 So. 2d 220, 223–24 (Miss. 1992) (holding that secret recordings by lawyers are usually ethical); *also Mississippi Bar v. Attorney ST*, 621 So. 2d 229, 232–33 (Miss. 1993) (holding that a lawyer who falsely denied to another that he was recording a telephone conversation violated Mississippi Rule 4.1, which tracks the Model Rule).)

Although secretly recording conversations with a third-party witness is legal and ethical in some jurisdictions, it is uncertain if secretly recording conversations with a client is ethical. A lawyer owes a duty of loyalty to the client not owed to a third-party witness. The ABA Standing Committee split on whether the Model Rules forbid a lawyer from secretly recording a conversation with a client concerning the subject matter of the representation. (ABA Formal Op. 01-422 (2001).) There is also a division in state ethics opinions addressing this issue. (*Compare* Idaho Formal Op. 130 (1989) (stating that client confidentiality promotes candor and sufficiently protects secret recording of client conversations), *with* Wisconsin E-94-5 (1994) (stating that fiduciary duties owed by a lawyer to a client require the client's consent to recording).) Because of the lack of unanimity within the Standing Committee on this issue, the ABA's position is that secret recording of client conversations is at least "inadvisable." (ABA Formal Op. 01-422 (2001).)

Conclusion

The law and ethics authorities dealing with a lawyer secretly recording a conversation vary from jurisdiction to jurisdiction. This variation reflects the underlying tension between the potential benefits to the client, the lawyer, and the legal system of such secret taping on the one hand and concern about candor and the image of the legal profession on the other.

Even in jurisdictions where secret recording is legal, it may still be unethical. And, where it is both legal and ethical, a lawyer is well advised not to deny that a recording is being made and to tread carefully when thinking about secretly recording conversations with clients.

Resources for Chapter 13

Rules and Standards

Model Rules of Professional Conduct 4.1, 4.4, 5.3, and 8.4.
Model Code of Professional Responsibility DR 1-102(A)(4).

Cases and Ethics Opinions

Attorney M. v. Mississippi, 621 So. 2d 220 (Miss. 1992).
Mississippi Bar v. Attorney ST, 621 So. 2d 229 (Miss. 1993).
ABA Formal Op. 337 (1974).
ABA Informal Op. 1320 (1975).
Idaho Formal Op. 130 (1989).
Ariz. Op. 90-02 (1990).
Wisconsin E-94-5 (1994).
ABA Formal Op. 01-422 (2001).

Articles, Reports, Books, and Other Sources

Douglas R. Richmond, *Deceptive Lawyering*, 74 U. Cin. L. Rev. 577 (2005).
Gerald B. Lefcourt, *Fighting Fire with Fire: Private Attorneys Using the Same Investigative Techniques as Government Attorneys: The Ethical and Legal Considerations for Attorneys Conducting Investigations*, 36 Hofstra L. Rev. 397 (2007).
18 U.S.C. § 2515.

CHAPTER 14

Brother's Keeper: Must You Protect Opponent's Confidentiality?

Lawyers usually think of the American legal system as adversarial and view legal ethics rules as reflecting that adversarial quality. But such a description is misleading. Both our legal system and our ethics rules are actually a blend of adversarial and cooperative elements.

Model Rule 3.3(a)(2) provides a simple but characteristic example. It states that "[a] lawyer shall not knowingly . . . fail to disclose to the tribunal legal authority in the controlling jurisdiction known to the lawyer to be directly adverse to the position of the client and not disclosed by opposing counsel." It imposes a cooperative duty to inform a state trial court of a directly adverse case or statute from that jurisdiction that the opponent has not already brought to the court's attention. But in regard to cases or statutes that are adverse to the lawyer's position but from another jurisdiction or not directly on point, the lawyer is allowed to take an adversarial approach, leaving it to the opposing lawyer or the court to find the adverse authority. Rule 3.3(a)(2) thus blends both cooperative and adversarial elements.

This chapter addresses the ethical question of whether a lawyer must adopt a cooperative or adversarial stance in regard to taking advantage of an opponent's inadvertent disclosure of confidential information. We do not address the closely related evidence issue of whether inadvertent disclosure constitutes a waiver of attorney-client privilege.

Confidentiality Basics

The obligation to protect client confidences is a cornerstone of legal ethics. Model Rule 1.6 directs that "[a] lawyer shall not reveal information relating to the representation of a client" and relieves the lawyer of this duty only if the client consents or an exception applies. Comment 3 to Model Rule 1.6 gives this obligation generous scope by providing that "[t]he confidentiality rule, for example, applies not only to matters communicated in confidence by the client but also to all information relating to the representation, whatever its source." The client is protected not only by Model Rule 1.6's ban on *revealing* client information, but also by Model Rule 1.8(b)'s restriction on *use* of client information other than revelation. Rule 1.8(b) states that "[a] lawyer shall not use information relating to representation of a client to the disadvantage of the client"—again, unless the client consents or certain exceptions apply.

Utilitarian reasoning underlies this protective attitude toward client information. If clients know that their information is protected from revelation or other use that may disadvantage them, they will freely consult with and fully disclose that information to their lawyers. In addition, confidentiality restrictions encourage lawyers to aggressively seek all information relevant to the legal issues confronting clients. The thinking here is that the more information lawyers have, the better they will advise and assist clients—better serving both clients and society.

The focus in confidentiality is almost exclusively on the lawyer's obligations in dealing with his or her own client's information. Model Rules 1.6 and 1.8(b) both center on the lawyer's handling of client information. The issues that most often put lawyer confidentiality in the spotlight deal with whether and when the lawyer's confidentiality obligation to a client should yield to the interests of the public or a third person. For example, proposals to allow a lawyer to reveal client information to remedy client fraud and prevent future client crime have regularly proved to be lightning rods for controversy.

Obligation to Another Lawyer's Client

What obligations, though, does a lawyer have to maintain the confidentiality of someone who is not his or her client, but the client of another lawyer, especially opposing counsel? Model Rules 1.6 and 1.8(b), the primary rules laying out the obligations of a lawyer regarding confidential information, are silent on what obligations an opposing lawyer may have toward the information that Rules 1.6 and 1.8(b) strive to protect.

A lawyer's potential receipt of an opposing client's confidential information is addressed most frequently in the context of the anticontact rule found in Model Rule 4.2. It provides that "[i]n representing a client, a lawyer shall not communicate about . . . the representation" with another lawyer's client. The anticontact rule, which has received great attention in both criminal and civil contexts, says nothing about what a lawyer should do upon receipt of an opposing client's information. But the rule's ban on one lawyer communicating with another lawyer's client is based in large part on preventing one lawyer from obtaining confidential information from the client of an opposing lawyer. The rule reflects the view that one lawyer should not be in possession of an opposing client's confidential information and that lawyers should restrict their conduct to reduce the risk of receiving such information. We discuss the anticontact rule in greater depth in the next chapter.

Inadvertent Disclosure of Confidential Information

The inadvertent disclosure of confidential client information by an opposing lawyer may occur in a number of ways, such as misdirecting a fax or e-mail, placing an item in the wrong envelope, or mistakenly producing a document during discovery. This issue has taken center stage in a series of ethics opinions and cases and appears in a number of professional responsibility teaching texts. Many states in recent years have adopted ethics rules specifically addressing inadvertent disclosure. The issue even appeared on prime-time television's *Law and Order* when a lawyer mistakenly sent prosecutor Jack McCoy an internal defense memorandum about an interview with a witness the defense did not plan to call.

In the face of mounting interest in inadvertent disclosure of confidential information and as a result of recommendations from the Ethics 2000 Commission, the ABA in 2002 amended Model Rule 4.4. Model Rule 4.4(b) now provides that "[a] lawyer who receives a document relating to the representation of the lawyer's client and knows or reasonably should know that the document was inadvertently sent shall promptly notify the sender." Comment 2 to Rule 4.4 defines "document" to include "e-mail or other electronic modes of transmission subject to being read or put into readable form." Interestingly, Rule 4.4(b) is not limited to documents protected by confidentiality or privilege. Comment 2 states that "[w]hether the lawyer is required to take additional steps, such as returning the original document, is a matter of law beyond the scope of these Rules. . . ." Comment 3 states that a lawyer may choose to return a mistakenly sent document "unread" and, when not required to do so by applicable law, "the decision to voluntarily return such a document is a matter of professional judgment ordinarily reserved to the lawyer."

In revising their ethics codes following the work of the ABA's Ethics 2000 Commission and the ABA's adoption of Model Rule 4.4(b), many states adopted ethics rules based on Model Rule 4.4(b). But in doing so, states have modified the rule so that substantial variation exists from state to state.

The Cooperative Approach

To place current Model Rule 4.4(b) in context, it is helpful to look back at the treatment of inadvertent disclosure that preceded MR 4.4(b). The ABA in Formal Opinion 92–368 (1992), which predated Model Rule 4.4(b) and was withdrawn in 2005 by Formal Opinion 05-437, originally took a clearly cooperative approach to the issue of a lawyer's obligations toward an opposing client's confidential information. The committee was asked to address the obligations of a lawyer who receives apparently confidential materials "under circumstances where it is clear that the materials were not intended for the receiving lawyer."

The committee concluded that the lawyer should: (1) not examine the materials once the error is discovered; (2) notify the sending lawyer; and (3) abide by the sending lawyer's instructions about what to do with the materials. These conclusions were based primarily on the importance of confidentiality—the view that confidentiality is so central to the attorney-client relationship that the opposing lawyer must cooperatively assist in remedying errors by an opposing lawyer that would undermine confidentiality. Despite the fact that the confidentiality rule itself reflects a highly adversarial stance, the committee ironically imposed a cooperative obligation on one lawyer to help another lawyer maintain that adversarial obligation.

The Adversarial Approach

Not all jurisdictions, however, adopted the cooperative approach. For example, in the year following the ABA's issuance of Opinion 92–368, a California appellate court expressed a dramatically different view of the appropriate response for a lawyer who receives inadvertently disclosed confidential information. Rather than refrain from examining or using the information, the court in *Aerojet-General Corp. v. Transport Indemnity Ins.*, 22 Cal. Rptr. 862 (1993), concluded that the lawyer's "professional obligation demands that he utilize his knowledge about the case on his client's behalf." (*Id.* at 867–68.) The court found no obligation to notify opposing counsel of his or her error. The Texas Supreme Court has also staked out a highly adversarial position on inadvertent disclosure, holding that "a lawyer [who] receives privileged materials because the opponent inadvertently produced them in discovery . . . ordinarily has no duty to notify the opponent or voluntarily return the materials." (*In re Meador*, 968 S.W.2d 346, 352 (Tex. 1998).)

Intermediate Positions

The original ABA position and the California view represent opposite poles—ABA Opinion 92-368 reflecting a highly cooperative approach and *Aerojet-General* a highly adversarial resolution to the problem of inadvertent disclosure. After the ABA published Opinion 92-368, ethics committees in some states followed its cooperative approach, whereas other states took a variety of positions between this approach and California's adversarial view. Illinois Opinion No. 98-04 (1999), for example, prescribes a cooperative or adversarial approach depending on the mental state of the receiving lawyer. If the receiving lawyer knows before examining a document that a mistake was made, the lawyer must follow the ABA cooperative prescription. The lawyer cannot examine or use the document and must notify the opposing lawyer and return the document. But if the lawyer has no such knowledge prior to examining the document, the lawyer is free to examine and use it.

Model Rule 4.4(b) reflects a different compromise between the cooperative and adversarial approaches, mandating notification but otherwise leaving the choice between cooperative and adversarial approach to the lawyer's discretion. After the ABA adopted Model Rule 4.4(b), states began addressing inadvertent disclosure through ethics rules rather than opinions.

Many states have now adopted some version of Model Rule 4.4(b). Some, such as Florida, adopted it verbatim, whereas others chose to modify it. The District of Columbia's Rule 4.4(b), for example, adopts the original ABA cooperative position of Opinion 92-368, stating that the lawyer who "knows, before examining the writing, that it has been inadvertently sent, shall not examine the writing, but shall notify the sending party and abide by the instructions of the sending party regarding the return or destruction of the writing." Louisiana and New Jersey have similar highly cooperative rules.

Maryland's Rule 4.4(b) is closer to Model Rule 4.4(b) than those found in the District of Columbia, Louisiana, and New Jersey, but the Maryland rule adds features not found in Model Rule 4.4(b). Maryland's rule is narrower and more adversarial than Model Rule 4.4(b) in that it applies only to information "protected from disclosure by statute or by an established evidentiary privilege" when the lawyer is "communicating with third persons." Model Rule 4.4(b) contains no such restrictions. But the Maryland rule appears broader and more cooperative than the Model Rule in that it mandates that a lawyer "shall not seek" protected information, shall "terminate the communication" of such information "immediately," and must give notice not only to the person whose information is entitled to protection but also to any relevant tribunal. North Dakota's rule uses the language of Model Rule 4.4(b), but adds an additional provision stating that the lawyer need not communicate or consult with the client regarding receipt or return of an inadvertently received document.

Although states divide on examination and use of the information at issue and on the need to return the document, almost all require notification. This makes sense for a number of reasons. Notification allows the opposing lawyer to challenge retention and use of the information in a timely fashion. The sending lawyer, for example, might ask a judge to resolve the matter. Judges are in a better position to do so than receiving lawyers because there is no risk that adversarial interest will cloud their judgment and they will have greater access to the facts surrounding the disclosure, having heard from both sides. Notification also keeps surprise from compounding the impact of the sending lawyer's error and resulting harm to the client, which may be significant. It also reduces the appearance of dishonesty in the receiving lawyer examining and using the information.

An Array of Rationales

Ethics committees and commentators who have addressed this issue have drawn on an array of rationales to support their positions. Those opting for the cooperative approach emphasize the importance of confidentiality not just to the lawyer's client, but to the overall administration of justice. By helping protect confidentiality for an opposing client, the receiving lawyer serves the interests of the justice system. Other values invoked in support of the cooperative view are the receiving lawyer's duty of honesty and courtesy to other lawyers as well as maintenance of the lawyers' public image. Finally, the cooperative view also appears to be based on a pragmatic concern about use of judicial time and resources. If the lawyer does not examine or use the information, notifies the sending lawyer, and returns the documents, there is not much left to fight about. If the lawyer retains and uses the documents, by contrast, the parties and both trial and appellate courts will likely spend time and resources arguing and resolving the factual, ethical, and legal issues presented at the time of the disclosure, at the time the receiving lawyer seeks to use them, and on appeal.

Some committees that adopted more adversarial approaches noted that the lawyer's confidentiality obligation runs to the client, not the opponent's client. Some also note the lack of any active wrongdoing on the receiving lawyer's part. Several point to the practical problem of "unringing the bell" once a lawyer has learned confidential information. Requiring a lawyer to purge his or her mind of such information, they point out, is a practical impossibility. Worse, they worry that a requirement that the lawyer not use the information could create a conflict of interest that might keep the lawyer from effectively serving the client.

Practical Implications

Regardless of whether a lawyer is inclined toward the cooperative or adversarial approach in handling inadvertently disclosed confidential information, the opinions, rules, and cases in this area suggest a number of practical implications.

First, lawyers should be careful to guard against accidental, as well as purposeful, disclosure of confidential information by themselves or others working in their offices. Model Rule 5.3 requires lawyers to take reasonable measures to ensure that nonlawyers comply with the professional obligations imposed on lawyers, such as confidentiality. A lawyer who fails to take reasonable steps to ensure that employees maintain client confidentiality may face professional discipline as well as a possible malpractice action.

Second, it is important to know the approach adopted in your jurisdiction because ethics opinions, rules, and case law vary from state to state. The logical starting point in acquiring such knowledge is finding out whether the relevant state has recently adopted a specific ethics rule addressing inadvertent disclosure, possibly modeled on Model Rule 4.4(b).

Third, although there is an increasing body of ethics opinions and rules, as well as case law, on this question, there is still a good chance that lawyers who find themselves in this position will not have any guidance in their jurisdictions. If in doubt about what to do with confidential information, taking an adversarial approach and examining and making use of the information run the risk of sanctions and disqualification. Following the cooperative approach reduces these risks. Alternatively, the lawyer can file the material under seal with the court and ask the judge to review it and provide guidance on the proper course of action.

Finally, the law of theft may apply to what is received. If the lawyer receives an errant fax or e-mail, it is unlikely to be considered "property" that could be the subject of theft. But if the item received is an original file, it may well be considered personal property. As a Maine ethics committee pointed out, it is a crime to retain mistakenly delivered property of another.

Resources for Chapter 14

Rules and Standards

Model Rules of Professional Conduct 1.6, 1.8(b), 3.3(a)(2), 4.2, and 4.4.
District of Columbia Rule of Professional Conduct 4.4(b).
Louisiana Rule of Professional Conduct 4.4(b).
Maryland Lawyer's Rule of Professional Conduct 4.4(b).
New Jersey Rule of Professional Conduct 4.4(b).

Cases and Ethics Opinions

Aerojet-General Corp. v. Transport Indemnity Ins., 22 Cal. Rptr. 862 (1993).
In re Meador, 968 S.W.2d 346 (Tex. 1998).
ABA Formal Opinion 92-368 (1992).
Illinois Opinion No. 98-04 (1999).
ABA Formal Opinion 05-437 (2005).

Articles, Reports, Books, and Other Sources

Trina Jones, *Inadvertent Disclosure of Privileged Information and the Law of Mistake: Using Substantive Legal Principles to Guide Ethical Decision Making*, 48 Emory L.J. 1255 (1999).
Andrew M. Perlman, *Untangling Ethics Theory from Attorney Conduct Rules: The Case of Inadvertent Disclosures*, 13 Geo. Mason L. Rev. 767 (2006).
Monroe Friedman, *Erroneous Disclosure of Damaging Information: A Response to Andrew Perlman*, 14 Geo. Mason L. Rev. 179 (2006).

CHAPTER 15

Anticontact Rule in Criminal Investigations

Confidentiality issues are magnets for attention, as evidenced by the series of corporate scandals that prompted changes to Model Rule 1.6 that now permit lawyers to disclose future client financial crime or fraud. Conflict of interest, the most heavily litigated subject area in legal ethics, also regularly draws interest from the public and lawyers. In comparison, the anticontact rule has a much lower public profile. Nor does it register brightly on the ethical radar screens of most lawyers. Indeed, many lawyers seem unaware that the rule exists.

Nonetheless, the anticontact rule has generated considerable controversy in the past two decades, especially its application to criminal investigations. In this chapter we examine the anticontact rule in the context of criminal investigations, its underlying policies, its application both to prosecutors and defense lawyers, and the debate that continues to surround the rule.

The Rule

Today either the Model Code or the Model Rules version of the anticontact rule has been adopted in each of the 50 states. The Model Rules current version, Rule 4.2, provides the following:

> In representing a client, a lawyer shall not communicate about the subject of the representation with a person the lawyer knows to be represented by another lawyer in the matter, unless the lawyer has the consent of the other lawyer or is authorized to do so by law or a court order.

The rule forbids a lawyer who is representing a client from communicating with the client of another lawyer regarding the representation. Its prohibition can be represented graphically as follows:

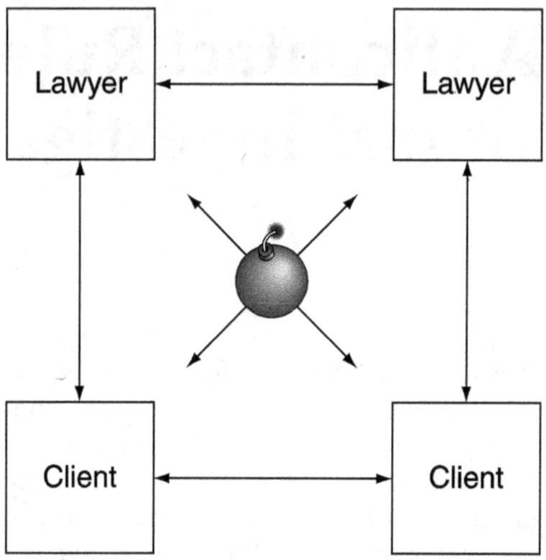

Communication is allowed along the sides of the square. One lawyer may communicate with the opposing lawyer, one client may communicate with the opposing client, and each lawyer may communicate with his or her own client. But communications between lawyer and opposing client diagonally across the square are generally forbidden.

The rule has a number of key features. The lawyer must know that another lawyer represents the person. Communication is barred only if it relates to "the subject matter of the representation." And only the opposing lawyer, not the client, may waive the protection of the rule.

One limiting feature worth noting is that the rule applies only if the lawyer is representing a client. Consider, for example, a situation in which a client represented by Lawyer A in a criminal matter is dissatisfied with Lawyer A and wishes to communicate with Lawyer B about replacing Lawyer A. May Lawyer B speak with Lawyer A's client? Comment [4] to the rule explains that because B is not "representing a client" at the time of the communication, the anticontact rule's prohibitions do not prevent Lawyer B from talking to A's client.

The rule also has a vicarious aspect. The Model Code's anticontact rule, DR 7-104(A)(1), specifies that a lawyer may not "cause another to communicate" with another lawyer's client under the same circumstances in which the attorney would himself or herself be barred from so communicating. The text of Model Rule 4.2 does not contain a similar explicit prohibition on communicating through another person. But the Model Rules achieve the same effect through Model Rules 5.3 and 8.4(a).

Model Rule 5.3 imposes on lawyers responsibilities for nonlawyers "employed or retained by or associated with a lawyer." Rule 5.3(b) requires a lawyer to "make reasonable efforts to ensure" that the conduct of such nonlawyers "is compatible with the professional obligations of the lawyer." And Rule 5.3(c) imposes responsibility on the lawyer for conduct of such nonlawyers "that would be a violation . . . if engaged in by a lawyer" if the lawyer orders or ratifies the offending conduct or, under certain circumstances, "fails to take reasonable remedial action." Model Rule 8.4(a) provides that "[i]t is professional misconduct for a lawyer to . . . violate . . . the Rules of Professional Conduct . . . through the acts of another."

This vicarious dimension of the anticontact rule has been the source of much of the controversy in applying the anticontact rule to prosecutors based on the actions of police and informants working with those prosecutors during criminal investigations, a subject we examine below.

Model Code DR 7-104(A)(1) is virtually identical in content to the current version of Model Rule 4.2 with one exception. The Model Code bars communication with a represented "party" rather than "person." Model Rule 4.2 used the word *party* until 1995, when *person* was substituted. Some had argued that use of the word *party* implied that the rule's protections attached only after the filing of an action, since a client does not become a party until an action is filed. The Model Rule's change of *party* to *person* clarifies the rule's applicability prior to the filing of an action as well as in nonlitigation contexts. Many states retain the word *party* in their anticontact rules, but courts have nonetheless found them applicable in the prefiling context.

Considerable attention has recently been focused on the question of the anticontact rule's application to corporate clients. The rule has uniformly been held to apply to corporate clients, though there is wide variation as to which employees of the corporation an opposing lawyer is barred from contacting under the rule. In an effort to bring consistency to identifying which employees are subject to the anticontact rule, Comment [7] explains that Rule 4.2 "prohibits communications with a constituent of the organization who supervises, directs, or regularly consults with the organization's lawyer concerning the matter or has authority to obligate the organization with respect to the matter, or whose act or omission in connection with the matter may be imputed to the organization for purposes of civil or criminal liability."

Potential sanctions for violating the anticontact rule include professional discipline, disqualification, and suppression. The use of suppression as a sanction has given courts increased occasion to address application of the anticontact rule in criminal investigations and fueled the growth in the last decade of case law on the subject.

Underlying Policies

Three primary rationales have traditionally been advanced in support of the anticontact rule. First, it protects a lawyer's client from "overreaching and deception" by an opposing lawyer. Second, the rule shields the relationship between a client and lawyer from interference by an opposing lawyer. Third, it helps guarantee that an opposing lawyer will not breach the confidentiality of a client's communications with his or her lawyer. (RESTATEMENT OF THE LAW GOVERNING LAWYERS § 158, cmt. b; ABA Comm. on Ethics and Prof'l Responsibility, Formal Op. 95-396 (1995).)

Courts have recognized that the anticontact rule also protects a "societal interest" that laypersons not make decisions with legal implications without the advice of their own lawyers, *United States v. Batchelor*, 484 F. Supp. 812 (E.D. Pa. 1980), and fosters "the internal integrity of and public confidence in the judicial system." (*United States v. Talao*, 222 F.3d 1133 (9th Cir. 2000).)

Not as frequently mentioned are the potential costs of the rule. It can hinder access to information by the client's adversary, especially when the adversary is a corporation. It may also hinder the prevention or remedying of client wrongdoing. Finally, it may hinder the prevention or remedying of unethical conduct by attorneys, such as conflict of interest or failing to keep a client informed.

Prosecutors

Police commonly use undercover agents or informants to gather information, including damaging admissions, from the target of an investigation. What if the prosecutor knows the subject of the investigation is represented by a lawyer in regard to the matter under investigation? Can the prosecutor nonetheless authorize the undercover agent or informant to communicate with the represented person?

Two powerful policy concerns militate against applying the rule to bar such undercover investigative activity. First, it would effectively insulate wealthy and sophisticated clients with retained counsel, such as corporate and white-collar criminals and those engaged in organized crime, from investigative techniques that are effective at unmasking their misdeeds. Second, because a prosecutor's involvement triggers the anticontact rule, it would discourage prosecutorial supervision of police investigations.

There are, however, cogent arguments in favor of applying the anticontact rule to police undercover contact with persons represented by lawyers. The idea of exempting prosecutors from a generally applicable legal ethics standard strikes many as unwise. It also seems unfair if defense counsel are not also exempted. Finally, it seems contrary to the plain language of the rule.

"Authorized by Law" Exception

The existence of these competing views helps explain the troubled history of the best known case to grapple with these issues, *United States v. Hammad*. In *United States v. Hammad*, 846 F.2d 854 (2d Cir. 1988), the Second Circuit originally held against a prosecutorial exemption. It reviewed the actions of a federal prosecutor who arranged for the undercover video and audio recording of an informant meeting with a represented person under criminal investigation. The court held that the prosecutor violated the anticontact rule by sending the informant to talk with the represented person. Concerned federal prosecutors in the Second Circuit petitioned for rehearing, which was denied. While a petition for hearing en banc was pending, the original panel issued another opinion on the matter, *United States v. Hammad*, 858 F.2d 834 (2d Cir. 1988), *cert. denied*, 498 U.S. 871 (1990).

In this final *Hammad* opinion, the Second Circuit held that the anticontact rule does not restrict the government from using informants against represented persons in a preindictment, noncustodial situation. The Second Circuit reasoned that "a prosecutor is 'authorized by law' to employ legitimate investigative techniques in conducting or supervising criminal investigations, and the use of informants to gather evidence against a suspect will frequently fall within the ambit of such authorization." (858 F.2d at 840.) The court, however, found that the prosecutor's use of a sham subpoena issued to the informant to help the informant surreptitiously gain the confidence of the represented suspect constituted misconduct.

After *Hammad*, there was a more than ten year running battle among the Department of Justice (DOJ), the Conference of Chief Justices representing all 50 state supreme courts, the ABA, disciplinary bodies, and others. The DOJ pushed for a rule change or separate rules to permit ex parte contacts with represented persons by government lawyers. Congress entered the fray by passing the Citizen Protection Act, known as the McDade Amendment, in 1998. The McDade Amendment provides the following:

> An attorney for the Government shall be subject to State laws and rules, and local Federal court rules, governing attorneys in each State where such attorney engages in that attorney's duties, to the same extent and in the same manner as other attorneys in that State.

Later, the U.S. Senate tried to repeal the McDade Amendment as part of the antiterrorism package passed in the aftermath of the September 11th attacks, but failed when the House of Representatives refused to include it in the Patriot Act of 2001. (28 U.S.C. § 530B(a).)

Current Law

Some courts have espoused a categorical approach finding that the anticontact rule does not apply in the investigative phase of a criminal case. It is triggered only with the commencement of adversarial proceedings. The Tenth Circuit, for example, in *United States v. Ryans*, 903 F.2d 731, 740 (10th Cir. 1990), held that the anticontact rule's "proscriptions do not attach during the investigative process before the initiation of criminal proceedings."

Following the lead of *Hammad*, though, most courts have rejected this categorical view and approached the application of the anticontact rule in criminal investigations on a case-by-case basis. Uniformly, these courts have held that prosecutorial use of an undercover agent or informant to communicate with someone known to be represented by counsel in the matter does not by itself violate the anticontact rule.

Outside the undercover agent/informant context, the meaning of the rule continues to evolve as courts respond to the nuances of particular factual contexts. Two recent cases are illustrative. Both find the anticontact rule applicable in the investigative context, but they differ on whether the rule was violated.

In *State v. Miller*, 600 N.W.2d 457 (Minn. 1999), the Minnesota Supreme Court dealt with the anticontact rule in the context of a 40-minute police interview of the defendant in the case, a corporate employee, during the execution of a search warrant at the corporation's place of business. The corporation's lawyer, having been notified that a search warrant was being executed, contacted the police by telephone, asked that no statements be taken from employees, and specifically asked to speak to the defendant. The police, upon advice of the prosecutor, refused to stop the interview or notify the defendant that the lawyer wanted to speak with him.

Despite the Minnesota anticontact rule's use of the word *party* rather than *person*, the court found that the rule applies prior to the filing of a formal charge and explicitly adopted a case-by-case approach to determining violations. The court found a violation and suppressed all statements taken after the lawyer asked the police to terminate the interview. The court interpreted the "authorized by law" exception to include "legitimate investigative processes" but not "a systematic isolation of the client from his attorney." (*Id.* at 468.)

United States v. Talao, 222 F.3d 1133 (9th Cir. 2000), applied California's version of the anticontact rule, as in *Miller*, in the context of an interview of a corporate employee. After receiving a subpoena to testify before a grand jury investigating her employer for false statements regarding employee wages and hours, the corporation's bookkeeper approached the prosecutor and said she was being pressured to give false testimony and did not want to be represented by the corporation's lawyer. The prosecutor informed the bookkeeper of her right to be represented by an attorney, but she declined. She then provided the prosecutor and case agent with information that she later recounted to the grand jury, including information about the possible destruction of corporate documents. Again, as in *Miller*, the corporation's lawyer became aware of the interview and demanded to speak with the bookkeeper. The prosecutor in *Talao*, however, unlike the prosecutor in *Miller*, informed the bookkeeper of the lawyer's presence and desire to speak with her, but the bookkeeper declined to speak with the lawyer.

After an indictment was returned against the corporation, it moved for dismissal on the basis of an anticontact rule violation. The trial judge denied the motion, but found that the prosecutor had violated the anticontact rule and stated that he would inform the jurors of the prosecutor's misconduct and instruct them to take it into account in assessing the bookkeeper's credibility.

The Ninth Circuit reversed. Endorsing the *Hammad* case-by-case approach, the court stated that the anticontact rule governed under circumstances "involving fully defined adversarial roles, impending grand jury proceedings, and awareness on the part of the responsible government actors" that the corporation was represented by counsel. (*Id.* at 1139.) Analogizing to the crime-fraud exception to the attorney-client privilege, the court stated that "it would be a perversion of the [anticontact rule] to extend it to protect corporate officers who would suborn perjury by their employees." (*Id.* at 1140.) The court emphasized the employee's initiation of the communication and the prosecutor's advising the employee of her right to counsel in finding no violation of the anticontact rule. (*Id.*)

Defense Counsel

Because controversy concerning the anticontact rule has focused on prosecutors, some might conclude that the anticontact rule has significance in criminal investigations only for prosecutors. Defense lawyers, though, should give thought to how the rule may affect them. Nothing in the text or comments to Rule 4.2 suggests that criminal defense lawyers are exempt from the rule. Indeed, ABA Formal Opinion 95-396 (1995) specifically states that "[d]efense counsel in criminal cases of course are . . . subject to the provisions of Rule 4.2."

Use of the word *party* in some versions of the anticontact rule might suggest that criminal defense lawyers are free to contact another lawyer's client if he or she has not been charged and thereby made a party to a criminal case. But courts, such as those in *Miller* and *Talao,* have rejected such a limitation when applying the rule to prosecutors and have construed the term *party* to encompass represented persons who have not been charged. And some jurisdictions, following the lead of the Model Rules as noted above, have replaced the word *party* with *person* in their anticontact rule.

A victim or complainant in a criminal case is normally not protected by the anticontact rule based on the relationship with the prosecutor because the prosecutor represents the government and not the victim or complainant. A Michigan ethics opinion, for example, approves of a defense lawyer contacting a complaining witness not represented by his or her own lawyer provided the lawyer makes it clear that the lawyer represents the defendant, does not give advice to the witness, and does not "request the witness to testify falsely or to refrain from giving information to the prosecutor or offer any inducement that is prohibited by law." (Michigan Bar Comm. on Prof'l & Judicial Ethics, RI-302 (1997).)

Due to the scarcity of reported cases and ethics opinions involving defense attorneys contacting uncharged represented persons during defense investigations, the precise contours of the anticontact rule as applied to criminal defense lawyers have yet to be determined.

Conclusion

Although the anticontact rule has a relatively low public profile, consequences for violating it can be severe. Failure to abide by the anticontact rule may lead to disqualification, suppression, or possible dismissal, or it may create grounds for appeal based on prosecutorial misconduct. Prosecutors and defense counsel may also face professional discipline for violating the anticontact rule.

Prosecutors and defense counsel must know how the anticontact rule in their jurisdiction is interpreted and applied. When in doubt, a prosecutor or defense lawyer may seek a clarifying court order, for example, to determine which employees of a represented corporation may be contacted. (*See In re Criminal Investigation of John Doe, Inc., et al.*, 194 F.R.D. 375 (D. Mass. 2000).) As with most ethics rules, proceeding cautiously when contacting or directing others to contact represented persons is the best policy.

Resources for Chapter 15

Rules and Standards

MODEL RULES OF PROFESSIONAL CONDUCT 4.2, 5.3, and 8.4(a).
MODEL CODE OF PROFESSIONAL RESPONSIBILITY DR 7-104(A)(1).

Cases and Ethics Opinions

United States v. Batchelor, 484 F. Supp. 812 (E.D. Pa. 1980).
United States v. Hammad, 846 F.2d 854 (2d Cir. 1988).
United States v. Hammad, 858 F.2d 834 (2d Cir. 1988), *cert. denied*, 498 U.S. 871 (1990).
United States v. Ryans, 903 F.2d 731 (10th Cir. 1990).
State v. Miller, 600 N.W.2d 457 (Minn. 1999).
In re Criminal Investigation of John Doe, Inc., et al., 194 F.R.D. 375 (D. Mass. 2000).
United States v. Talao, 222 F.3d 1133 (9th Cir. 2000).
ABA Comm. on Ethics and Prof'l Responsibility, Formal Op. 95-396 (1995).
Michigan Bar Comm. on Prof'l & Judicial Ethics, RI-302 (1997).

Articles, Reports, Books, and Other Sources

William H. Edmonson, *A "New" No-Contact Rule: Proposing an Addition to the No-Contact Rule to Address Questioning of Suspects after Unreasonable Charging Delays*, 80 N.Y.U. L. REV. 1773 (2005).

Ben Kempinen, *The Ethics of Prosecutor Contact with the Unrepresented Defendant*, 19 GEO. J. LEGAL ETHICS 1147 (2006).

18 U.S.C. § 530 B (2000) (commonly called the McDade Amendment).

RESTATEMENT OF THE LAW GOVERNING LAWYERS § 158.

CHAPTER 16

Destroying Documents

Destruction of documents relating to possible white-collar criminal and civil wrongdoing has received much attention. Arthur Andersen's destruction of documents relating to the Enron scandal, as well as the prosecution of former Credit Suisse First Boston investment banker Frank Quattrone on an obstruction of justice charge related to e-mail purging, were both well publicized. Lawyers involved in destroying documents or counseling such destruction face potential criminal liability and damage to reputation, but destruction also raises ethical issues. This chapter addresses the ethical and legal issues implicated in document destruction, both paper and electronic.

Client destruction of documents raises a host of potential ethics issues. Conflict of interest issues may arise, for example, because a lawyer's potential exposure to criminal liability and ethics sanctions creates tension between the client's right to be informed about the limits of obstruction statutes and the lawyer's interest in avoiding allegations or charges of engaging in, assisting, or counseling illegal activity. Is the lawyer advising a client against destroying documents because it is illegal and not in the client's best interest? Or is the lawyer being overly restrictive only to avoid questions about his or her own conduct?

The ethical obligation of confidentiality may also be implicated. When a lawyer learns that a client has destroyed or intends to destroy documents in violation of a criminal obstruction statute, that knowledge is "information relating to the representation" under Model Rule 1.6. But does it fall within a recognized confidentiality exception? Model Rule 1.6(b)(5) allows a lawyer to reveal information "to establish a defense to a criminal charge . . . against the lawyer based upon conduct in which the client was involved, or to respond to allegations in any proceeding concerning the lawyer's representation of the client. . . ." A lawyer may reveal confidential client information, such as communication regarding document destruction, if the lawyer faces criminal liability on the basis of having performed, assisted, or counseled the activity. Comment [10] to Model Rule 1.6 states that a lawyer does not have to wait for criminal charges to be filed, but may reveal the information as soon as "an assertion of . . . complicity" in client wrongdoing is made.

Model Rule 1.4(b) requires that a lawyer "explain a matter to the extent reasonably necessary to permit the client to make informed decisions. . . ." The lawyer may find this obligation difficult to fulfill because it is likely that the client will not seek counsel before destroying documents. Even if the client does seek counsel, the client may be unwilling to listen to the lawyer's advice.

Though client destruction of documents implicates an array of ethics concerns, this chapter focuses on Model Rule 1.1's obligation of competence and Model Rule 3.4(a)'s duty to avoid obstructing access to evidence.

Model Rule 1.1 states that "[a] lawyer shall provide competent representation to a client. Competent representation requires the legal knowledge, skill, thoroughness and preparation reasonably necessary for the representation." Counseling clients about document destruction is particularly challenging due to complexity and ambiguity in the law on both the federal and state levels.

Complexity, Ambiguity, and Variability

The criminal law relating to document destruction—typically obstruction of justice statutes—is complicated. There are several federal statutes, the applicability of which depends on the sort of legal proceeding in which the documents might be used. (*See* 18 U.S.C. §§ 401, 1503, 1505, and 1512.) These statutes pose difficult interpretation issues, such as determining the starting point for liability, the mental states required for conviction, and the potential relevance of the destroyed documents to the legal proceeding, sometimes referred to as a nexus requirement.

The law also suffers from ambiguity. At times the federal statutes are silent on key issues, leaving it to the courts to articulate and define offense elements. In addition, the applicable criminal law underwent change when Congress added provisions in the wake of the Enron scandal, in which accountants destroyed relevant documents. The contours of these new provisions have yet to be clearly demarcated.

Finally, and perhaps most important, federal statutes often vary from state statutes, and state statutes vary widely from jurisdiction to jurisdiction on issues such as the point at which criminal liability begins. Many business activities in white-collar corruption cases implicate both federal and state laws, as the investigations and prosecutions conducted by then New York Attorney General Eliot Spitzer illustrate. Often, white-collar wrongdoing impacts more than one state. (*See Legal Ethics and the Destruction of Evidence*, 88 YALE L.J. 1665 (1979), for a useful overview of the variety found in state obstruction laws.)

Underestimating Reach and Impact

Often clients, in-house counsel, and lawyers advising white-collar clients appear unaware of the actual reach of obstruction statutes and conclude that liability cannot attach until the client has been served with a subpoena or document request, or until a pleading commencing a legal action has been filed. Neither generalization is valid.

Model Penal Code § 241.7, for example, provides that "[a] person commits a misdemeanor if, believing that an official proceeding or investigation is pending *or about to be instituted*, he . . . alters, destroys, conceals, or removes any record, document, or thing with purpose to impair its verity or availability in such proceedings or investigation" (emphasis added). And once a federal government inquiry has started, the Sarbanes-Oxley Act provides that knowingly altering, destroying, or concealing any document "with the intent to impede, obstruct, or influence the investigation" is a federal offense carrying a sentence of up to 20 years. (18 U.S.C. § 1519 (2002).)

Clients and lawyers also may miscalculate their chances of destroying documents undiscovered. Under the pressure of time and panicked by the prospect of legal liability and/or job loss, some individuals find the ease and speed of destroying files an irresistible temptation. But e-mail often remains on the servers of both senders and recipients, and deleted electronic documents are usually recoverable from the computer's hard drive by means of forensic software programs. In addition, the recipients of these e-mails or files may have retained a copy or sent one to a third party. Similarly, paper documents, even when originals are shredded, can be traced through photocopies, data on the computer that created the printed files, or other documents that refer to the shredded documents.

In addition to miscalculating their chances of destroying documents undiscovered, clients and lawyers may not fully grasp the potential consequences of document destruction. Once discovered, the government can file an obstruction charge *in addition* to charges related to the underlying wrongdoing. Filing an obstruction charge makes it easier for the prosecutor to admit evidence of destruction in a case based primarily on the underlying wrongdoing. Obstruction charges may also be filed *instead* of charges concerning the underlying wrongdoing, because obstruction is often easier for the prosecution to prove and the jury to understand than charges relating to the original wrongdoing, such as complicated fraud charges.

Evidence of document destruction has been found admissible in both criminal and civil cases, even without a charge of obstruction, and may prove useful as circumstantial evidence of the underlying wrongdoing. Prosecutors may argue, and jurors may draw, a more damning inference about the content of a missing document than the actual document would have supported.

Document destruction also gives the prosecutor leverage in negotiating a guilty plea or recruiting witnesses to make the government's case. If discovered, such actions may have a lasting impact on the professional reputation of a person or organization. Finally, as the Arthur Andersen case illustrates, such actions may jeopardize the very existence of an organization. The Supreme Court's reversal of the Andersen conviction provides scant vindication for an entity that effectively collapsed during the government challenge to the company's document destruction procedures.

Obstructing Access to Evidence; Wrongdoing by Employees

Model Rule 3.4(a) states that "[a] lawyer shall not . . . unlawfully obstruct another party's access to evidence or unlawfully alter, destroy or conceal a document or other material having potential evidentiary value. A lawyer shall not counsel or assist another person to do such an act. . . ."

A key word in this provision is *unlawfully*. The ethics provision incorporates legal standards controlling obstruction of justice, and, in doing so, Rule 3.4(a) incorporates the complexity, ambiguity, and variability of the multiple laws that apply to destruction of evidence.

The ethics rule may impose a greater duty than the underlying laws to which it refers. Note that the protection afforded by this section extends not only to items that would be admissible, but also to items having "potential evidentiary value."

Model Rule 1.13 deals with a lawyer's responsibility upon learning of wrongdoing by a corporate employee. If a lawyer disagrees with a decision to destroy documents and concludes that it violates the law, this ethics rule offers a road map of options that the lawyer may pursue within the corporation to try to change the decision in order to protect the best interest of the corporation.

Conclusion

The law and ethics of document destruction are often complicated. Nonetheless, examining them provides a few clear lessons for both lawyers and their clients. First, the duty to preserve documents is triggered no later than the commencement of litigation, and in some instances even earlier. If there is a government inquiry, federal law prohibits destruction, alteration, or concealment of documents; many state laws have similar provisions. Hence, even routine document destruction policies should be suspended once a government inquiry is started. Second, if documents or computer files are destroyed or altered, the original versions stand a good chance of being discovered in an investigation. Third, a lawyer must know the applicable federal and state laws when advising clients about document destruction in order to avoid violations of the law by both client and lawyer, but also because the ethics rules in this area incorporate legal standards in defining ethical obligations.

Resources for Chapter 16

Rules and Standards

Model Rules of Professional Conduct 1.1, 1.4(b), 1.6(b)(5), 1.13, and 3.4(a).

Model Penal Code § 241.7.

18 U.S.C. §§ 401, 1503, 1505, 1512, and 1519.

Articles, Reports, Books, and Other Sources

Legal Ethics and the Destruction of Evidence, 88 Yale L.J. 1665 (1979).

Dana E. Hill, *Anticipatory Obstruction of Justice: Pre-Emptive Document Destruction Under the Sarbanes-Oxley Anti-Shredding Statute, 18 U.S.C. 1519*, 89 Cornell L. Rev. 1519 (2004).

Stuart P. Green, *Uncovering the Cover-Up Crimes*, 42 Am. Crim. L. Rev. 9 (2005).

Albert D. Spalding Jr. & Mary Ashby Morrison, *Criminal Liability for Document Shredding After Arthur Andersen LLP*, 43 Am. Bus. L.J. 647 (2006).

CHAPTER 17

Implicit Plea Agreements and Issues of Disclosure

Prosecutors have a legal and an ethical obligation to disclose to the defendant plea agreements entered into to gain the cooperation of a key witness. Defense counsel typically uses the disclosed deal to argue that the cooperating witness's testimony is unreliable because the agreement gives the witness an incentive to fabricate. But what happens if the prosecutor makes only vague comments the witness views as implying a reward of leniency? Is there an agreement if the witness offers to testify to gain a benefit and the prosecutor gives encouragement but no definite promise? If a prosecutor gives a witness lenient treatment after the witness testifies, should a court conclude that there was an implicit agreement that should have been disclosed? In this chapter, we review the law and ethics of prosecutorial disclosure and discuss various approaches courts take in answering these questions.

Legal Disclosure Obligation

Giglio v. United States, 405 U.S. 150 (1972), is the leading case on disclosure of impeachment material. In *Giglio*, the defendant contended that the government failed to disclose a promise of immunity in return for testimony from a key witness. Although the government contested whether such a promise was made, the Supreme Court assumed it had and held that such an agreement must be disclosed.

Some read *Giglio* narrowly that a prosecutor's disclosure obligation extends only to agreements made with key witnesses. But

Giglio describes the obligation as encompassing more than agreements: "When the 'reliability of a given witness may well be determinative of guilt or innocence,' nondisclosure of evidence *affecting credibility* falls within . . . [*Brady*'s] general rule." (405 U.S. at 154.) (Emphasis added.)

The language of later Supreme Court opinions reflects this broader view of *Giglio*. *Strickler v. Greene*, 527 U.S. 263, 281–82 (1999), states that disclosure is required when evidence is "favorable to the accused, either because it is exculpatory, or because it is *impeaching*." (Emphasis added.) A more recent opinion, *U.S. v. Ruiz*, 536 U.S. 622, 628 (2002), cites *Giglio* for the proposition that "exculpatory evidence includes 'evidence *affecting*' *witness* '*credibility*.'" (Emphasis added.) Lower federal courts also read *Giglio* broadly as covering impeachment material such as prior inconsistent statements, prior false testimony, and government facilitation of a witness's illegal drug use.

A current division of opinion among federal courts about disclosure of alleged implicit plea agreements with government witnesses results in part from these courts adopting differing interpretations of *Giglio*. Some appear to read the case narrowly as requiring disclosure only of agreements. Others interpret it broadly to apply to any impeaching evidence, including but not limited to agreements.

Ethical Disclosure Obligation

The ABA Model Rules of Professional Conduct require the prosecutor to "make timely disclosure to the defense of all evidence or information known to the prosecutor that tends to negate the guilt of the accused or mitigates the offense. . . ." (Model Rule 3.8(d).) Prosecution Function Standard 3-3.11 of the ABA Criminal Justice Standards similarly requires timely disclosure of "all evidence or information which tends to negate the guilt of the accused or mitigate the offense charged or which would tend to reduce the punishment of the accused."

The ethical standard requires disclosure of *all evidence* that tends to negate guilt or mitigate the offense. Because there is no materiality requirement, it is more expansive than the constitutional standard. (*See Kyles v. Whitley*, 514 U.S. 419 (1995) (noting that the Constitution "requires less of the prosecutor" than Model Rule 3.8(d) or the ABA Criminal Justice Standards).)

Disciplinary cases demonstrate that the ethical obligation extends to all evidence regarding the credibility of a witness, not just agreements. For example, in *People v. Mucklow*, 35 P.3d 527 (Colo. 2000), the Colorado Supreme Court publicly censured an assistant prosecutor for failing to disclose impeaching evidence in the form of a prior inconsistent statement. In another case, *In re Jordan*, 913 So. 2d 775 (La. 2005), the Louisiana Supreme Court disciplined a prosecutor who failed to disclose a witness's statement that conflicted with two other statements from the same witness. (*Id.* at 779.) In reaching its decision, the Louisiana Supreme Court noted that *Giglio* requires disclosure of "evidence which impeaches the testimony of a witness whose credibility or reliability may determine guilt or innocence." (*Id.* at 782.)

Judicial Approaches to Implicit Plea Agreements

Cases dealing with disclosure of alleged implicit plea agreements reveal that courts struggle with defining the scope of the prosecutor's disclosure obligation regarding impeachment. Some appear to view *Giglio* as requiring disclosure only of impeachment evidence in the form of an agreement to gain testimony. Others read *Giglio* broadly to require disclosure of all impeachment evidence.

A Sixth Circuit case, *Bell v. Bell*, 460 F.3d 739 (6th Cir. 2006), *vacated, reh'g granted en banc*, No. 04-5523, 2006 U.S. App. LEXIS 32575 (6th Cir. Dec. 15, 2006), exemplifies the problems a court confronts if *Giglio* is read narrowly. In *Bell*, the defendant filed a federal habeas corpus petition alleging a violation of the prosecutor's disclosure obligation. A key government witness was a jailhouse informant who testified that the defendant admitted having shot and killed a man. The informant testified that the defendant also admitted having shot and killed the man's wife after she saw the defendant kill her husband. The informant's testimony contradicted the defendant's claim that he was not the killer and also provided an evidentiary basis for the jury to find premeditation with respect to the killing of the wife. The defense admitted into evidence the fact that the informant witness had an upcoming parole hearing and argued to the jury that this fact was a reason to disregard the witness's testimony because it gave him a reason to lie. The prosecutor argued that "he did not have any 'say-so' with the parole board." (*Id.* at 746–47.) The jury apparently relied on the witness's testimony and convicted the defendant of first-degree murder of the wife and second-degree murder of her husband. The defendant received a life sentence and a 20-year sentence, running consecutively.

In the defendant's habeas petition, he argued that *Brady* material had been withheld. He pointed to three pieces of evidence the prosecution did not disclose: (1) the witness approached the prosecution offering to testify in exchange for a transfer of facilities or work release; (2) shortly after speaking with the witness, the prosecutor nolle prosequied two counts of grand larceny and two counts of concealing stolen property as part of a plea deal in which the witness received concurrent sentences for two counts of concealing stolen property; and (3) the prosecutor wrote a letter to the parole board on behalf of the witness after the defendant's trial. The defendant argued that such evidence was subject to disclosure because it could have been used to impeach the key witness and was material because the witness was the only source of evidence of premeditation for the first-degree murder conviction.

The prosecution argued that the impeachment evidence was not subject to disclosure because the defendant failed to show an agreement between the witness and the prosecution. The prosecution's position was premised on a narrow reading of *Giglio*—that evidence of an *agreement* regarding leniency with a government witness is the only type of impeachment evidence subject to *Brady* disclosure. The Sixth Circuit appeared to adopt the prosecution's view that impeachment disclosure under *Giglio* is limited to agreements between a prosecutor and a witness. But the court nonetheless held against the government in the *Bell* case, reasoning that if a "witness approached the prosecution to testify with the expectation of some benefit, and . . . the prosecution understood this expectation and fulfilled the expectation by actually bestowing some benefit," then the defendant "has sufficiently demonstrated a tacit agreement that must be disclosed under *Brady*." (460 F.3d at 754.)

In finding the existence of a tacit agreement, the Sixth Circuit relied primarily on four factors. First, the prosecutor's notes of the first meeting with the witness indicated that the witness wanted some benefit in exchange for his testimony, and that a transfer of facilities or work release was discussed. Second, at the habeas evidentiary hearing the prosecutor stated that he was aware that the witness expected something in exchange for the information. Third, the court noted that shortly after the witness agreed to testify against the defendant the prosecutor gave a benefit to the witness by dropping four charges against the witness. Finally, the court noted that the letter to the parole board after the trial stated that the prosecutor was requesting an early parole of the witness "[b]ased on cooperation" of the witness. The court characterized the phrase "[b]ased on cooperation" as evidence of a "*quid pro quo*" of the witness's testimony in exchange for the prosecutor's letter.

In essence, the *Bell* court reached the proper result of requiring disclosure, but did so in an unfortunate and unnecessarily convoluted way, by distorting the meaning of the word *agreement*. Evidence of a witness's expectation of a reward for testimony is clearly relevant to bias. Evidence of a witness's fear of some negative consequence of not testifying, such as physical harm or financial loss or prosecution of a family member, is also clearly relevant to bias. If evidence of fear or expectation of reward is material, it should be disclosed under *Giglio* as impeachment evidence. But that does not mean that such expectation or fear constitutes an agreement. The word *agreement* in both legal and common usage requires some sort of "meeting of the minds." A witness may have expectations or fears with or without reaching an agreement with the prosecutor. This remains true even if the witness after testifying receives an expected or hoped for reward or avoids a feared negative consequence. Although expectation and later reward are circumstantial evidence—even powerful circumstantial evidence—of an agreement, they do not themselves constitute an agreement. The *Bell* court's apparent narrow reading of *Giglio* seems to have led the court to distort the meaning of *agreement* in order to require disclosure of obviously relevant impeachment evidence regarding bias.

In focusing on whether an agreement was explicit or implicit, the prosecutor and Sixth Circuit read *Giglio* narrowly as applying only to agreements and not broadly to apply to impeaching evidence. If the Sixth Circuit had interpreted *Giglio* broadly, it could have found that the first two pieces of evidence—that the witness approached the prosecution offering to testify in exchange for a transfer of facilities or work release, and that the prosecutor dismissed four felony counts as part of a plea deal shortly after speaking with the witness—should have been disclosed as impeachment evidence even if there was no agreement. Other circuits have also unwisely read *Giglio* to require an agreement before triggering the *Brady* disclosure obligation in the area of impeachment.

The Eighth Circuit, though, has read *Giglio* broadly. In *Reutter v. Solem*, 888 F.2d 578 (8th Cir. 1989), the court found a *Brady* violation based on the prosecution's failure to disclose the impending commutation hearing of the key government witness and that the prosecutor was one of three members of the commutation board who would consider the witness's commutation request. The district court found that there was no agreement between the witness and the prosecutor, and therefore no disclosure obligation. The Eighth Circuit reversed, holding that whether disclosure of impeaching evidence is required "does not depend on a finding of either an express or an implied agreement" between the government's witness and the prosecutor. (*Id.* at 582.)

In our view, the Eighth Circuit has taken the better approach. Interpreting *Giglio* narrowly to require an agreement is unwise for several reasons. First, requiring an agreement potentially excludes critical impeachment evidence from disclosure and is contrary to both the language and spirit of Supreme Court precedent on *Brady* disclosure. Second, requiring an agreement pressures courts, such as the Sixth Circuit in *Bell*, to distort the meaning of *agreement* and to equate circumstantial evidence of an agreement with an agreement. Distorting language by giving a word such as *agreement* a meaning in the disclosure context that differs from both its legal meaning in other contexts and its meaning in common usage invites confusion and undermines transparency in criminal law. Finally, this view of the legal disclosure obligation ignores the fact that the prosecutor's ethical duty to disclose impeachment evidence is not limited to prosecutorial agreements with witnesses.

Resources for Chapter 17

Rules and Standards

Model Rule of Professional Conduct 3.8(d).

ABA Criminal Justice Standards for the Prosecution Function, Standard 3-3.11.

Cases and Ethics Opinions

Giglio v. United States, 405 U.S. 150 (1972).

Reutter v. Solem, 888 F.2d 578 (8th Cir. 1989).

Kyles v. Whitley, 514 U.S. 419 (1995).

Strickler v. Greene, 527 U.S. 263 (1999).

People v. Mucklow, 35 P.3d 527 (Colo. 2000).

U.S. v. Ruiz, 536 U.S. 622 (2002).

In re Jordan, 913 So. 2d 775 (La. 2005).

Bell v. Bell, 460 F.3d 739 (6th Cir. 2006), *vacated, reh'g granted en banc*, No. 04-5523, 2006 U.S. App. LEXIS 32575 (6th Cir. Dec. 15, 2006).

Articles, Reports, Books, and Other Sources

Eli Paul Mazur, *Rational Expectations of Leniency: Implicit Plea Agreements and the Prosecutor's Rule as a Minister of Justice*, 51 Duke L.J. 1333 (2002).

R. Michael Cassidy, *"Soft Words of Hope": Giglio, Accomplice Witnesses, and the Problem of Implied Inducements*, 98 Nw. U.L. Rev. 1129 (2004).

PART 7

Plea Negotiations

CHAPTER 18

Disclosing Exculpatory Material in Plea Negotiations

Are prosecutors constitutionally compelled to disclose exculpatory material to criminal defendants who plead guilty? Are they ethically bound to do so? Consider a hypothetical robbery prosecution in which the victim identifies the defendant from police photos of known offenders. Because the victim's identification is strong and the offense violent, the prosecutor refuses to enter into plea negotiations. A week before trial, the victim is apprehensive about the trial and the prospect of cross-examination. She tells the prosecutor that she fears she made a mistake in the photo identification and now thinks the man she picked from the police photos is not the man who robbed her. May the prosecutor negotiate a guilty plea without disclosing the victim's statement about her possible misidentification of the defendant? What if the victim tells the prosecutor she is certain the man she picked is not the man who robbed her?

Despite the fact that more than 90 percent of federal and state criminal cases are resolved through guilty pleas, the prosecutor's disclosure obligations regarding exculpatory material in plea negotiations remain controversial. This chapter examines the history, development, and current state of the law on prosecutorial disclosure of exculpatory material in plea negotiations and discusses both practical and ethical implications for defense lawyers and prosecutors. It also argues that such disclosure should be constitutionally mandated.

History

Over 40 years ago, the Supreme Court held in *Brady v. Maryland*, 373 U.S. 83 (1963), that due process requires a prosecutor to disclose material exculpatory evidence to a defendant. In subsequent cases, the Supreme Court refined the *Brady* doctrine. In *Giglio v. United States*, 405 U.S. 150 (1972), for example, the Court expanded the scope of the *Brady* rule by holding that impeachment evidence falls within the *Brady* disclosure requirement. Later, though, the Court significantly limited the *Brady* rule by imposing a narrow definition of materiality. In *United States v. Bagley*, 473 U.S. 667, 682 (1985), the Court explained that evidence in the hands of the government is material "only if there is a reasonable probability that, had the evidence been disclosed to the defense, the result of the proceedings would have been different."

Despite the long history of the *Brady* rule, the Supreme Court was slow to address the question of whether the constitutional mandate of *Brady* applies in the context of plea negotiations. All but one of the Supreme Court cases interpreting and applying the *Brady* rule have involved convictions obtained by means of a trial. We address the single case involving a guilty plea later in this chapter.

Ethical Disclosure Obligation

In addition to their legal discovery duty, prosecutors have an ethical obligation to turn over exculpatory material. Rule 3.8 of the ABA's Model Rules of Professional Conduct, adopted in almost every state, provides the following:

> The prosecutor in a criminal case shall . . . make timely disclosure to the defense of all evidence or information known to the prosecutor that tends to negate the guilt of the accused or mitigates the offense, and, in connection with sentencing, disclose to the defense and to the tribunal all unprivileged mitigating information known to the prosecutor, except when the prosecutor is relieved of this responsibility by a protective order of the tribunal.

The precursor to Rule 3.8, Disciplinary Rule 7-103(B) of the ABA Model Code of Professional Responsibility, sets forth a similar obligation.

The prosecutor's ethical disclosure duty is broader than the constitutional duty under *Brady*. The Supreme Court in *Kyles v. Whitley,* 514 U.S. 419, 432 (1995), acknowledged the more expansive nature of the ethical requirement, stating that *Brady* "requires less than . . . ABA Model Rule of Professional Conduct 3.8(d)." The ethics rule, unlike the *Brady* rule, has no materiality restriction and is not limited to admissible evidence.

The ethics rule makes no specific mention of plea negotiations or guilty pleas. But the language of the rule, in particular its requirement of "timely disclosure," certainly appears to mandate that prosecutors disclose exculpatory material during plea negotiations, if not sooner. Yet, secondary sources, such as treatises, do not typically discuss the ethics rule in the context of plea negotiations, and we have found no ethics authority that applies the rule in that context.

Because their attention tends to focus on *Brady's* constitutional mandate, prosecutors may not be aware of the ethics rule and the fact that it requires more than *Brady*. Even if they are aware of the ethics rule, prosecutors may fail to perceive its message because of the legal profession's general attitude toward disclosure of information in negotiations. Disclosure of material information is a central issue in negotiation ethics. A number of commentators have argued for a duty of disclosure of information material to a matter in the context of all negotiations, but the Model Rules have not adopted such a rule. Model Rule 4.1 states that "a lawyer shall not knowingly . . . make a false statement of material fact or law to a third person," but nondisclosure appears to be an accepted convention for negotiators. Many seasoned defense attorneys and prosecutors accordingly expect each other to play their cards close to the vest unless there is a rule or decision to the contrary. These attitudes present the danger that prosecutors will draw the line between ethical and unethical behavior regarding exculpatory material by reference to prevailing practice standards accepting nondisclosure in negotiations rather than the language of Model Rule 3.8(d).

For federal prosecutors in particular, the tendency to be less than forthcoming about the weaknesses in their cases in plea negotiations is buttressed by the fact that prosecutors do not have an affirmative duty to turn over impeachment evidence concerning their witnesses under the Jenck's Act and Federal Rule of Criminal Procedure 26.2 unless and until the witness testifies at trial. Pursuant to state discovery rules, state prosecutors in many jurisdictions, however, have a more extensive disclosure obligation at earlier phases in the case than their federal counterparts and, thus, may be more likely to recognize and respond to the ethical disclosure mandate.

Implicit Brady *Waivers*

The *Brady* rule is familiar to prosecutors and defense counsel alike. Every day in state and federal trial courts, defense counsel request and prosecutors agree to provide *Brady* material as a routine part of pretrial motion practice. When, as often happens, the case is resolved through a negotiated plea, however, typically nothing is said about *Brady* material. Federal and state rules of criminal procedure covering plea allocution do not mention a defendant's right to *Brady* material. And *Brady* disclosure is not usually listed in the litany of rights the defendant is told he or she is waiving when entering a guilty plea.

Defense lawyers tend to assume that a defendant has the constitutional right to receive *Brady* material prior to entry of a guilty plea. Prosecutors often view the defendant's decision to plead guilty as extinguishing any such right—that receipt of *Brady* material is a trial right relinquished along with the right to a trial by pleading guilty.

Why Require Disclosure of Exculpatory Information During Plea Negotiations?

DNA testing has provided vivid lessons on wrongful convictions, and the consequent exonerations reveal a host of sources contributing to inaccuracy in criminal trials, such as the use of jailhouse informants, eyewitness identification error, inadequate legal representation, coerced confessions, and the psychological phenomenon of escalation of commitment toward the guilt of a particular suspect. The same factors increase the risk of convicting the innocent through guilty pleas. Another factor associated with wrongful convictions is prosecutorial failure to reveal exculpatory information in violation of *Brady*.

Is there reason to believe that failure to disclose *Brady* material contributes to factually inaccurate guilty pleas? Failure to disclose exculpatory information unknown to the defense at trial obviously means the jury will not hear the evidence and be more likely to render an inaccurate verdict. But there is no jury at a guilty plea hearing.

An intuitive response to the question of whether *Brady* disclosure aids accuracy in guilty pleas is "no." Two assumptions prompt such a response. First, it is appealing to assume that a defendant entering a guilty plea, unlike a juror at a trial, knows whether or not he or she "did it." A second assumption is that a defendant is very unlikely to make a false inculpatory statement when entering a guilty plea in open court. After all, the defendant clearly knows that factual statements admitting guilt in a guilty plea hearing are against the defendant's penal and social interests, having been warned by the judge that an admission of guilt at the hearing will provide the basis for a criminal conviction. In addition, a defendant makes such statements after receiving advice of counsel and often under oath and subject to penalty of perjury.

Undoubtedly *most* defendants who plead guilty know the facts determining their criminal liability, and they are also sincere when they confess their guilt in a guilty plea. In the pages that follow, though, we demonstrate two things: (1) some defendants pleading guilty lack such knowledge and sincerity, and (2) we need to examine critically our assumptions about the knowledge and sincerity of defendants pleading guilty. Once we understand the knowledge and sincerity risks posed during guilty pleas, we can see how *Brady* disclosure in the guilty plea context would help reduce those risks.

Knowledge

The notion that a defendant knows whether or not he or she "did it"—that is, whether or not the defendant engaged in an act that fulfills the conduct element of the charged offense—is certainly true in most cases. But it is not true in all cases. Moreover, even if a defendant knows whether or not he or she fulfilled the act element of the offense, it does not necessarily follow that the defendant has adequate knowledge to establish other elements of the crime or other factors critical in determining criminal liability. The view that a defendant knows if he or she "did it" reflects a restricted, simplistic view of guilt and innocence that ignores many of the factors our substantive criminal law uses to define criminal liability, such as circumstances, results, causation, mental states, and defenses.

Two cases exemplify knowledge deficiencies. The defendant in *State v. Gardner*, 855 P.2d 1144 (Idaho Ct. App. 1994), was charged with vehicular manslaughter after the car he was driving crossed the center line of a highway and ran into an oncoming truck, killing one person and seriously injuring three others. Tests indicated that Gardner was under the influence of marijuana and sleep deprived. Gardner pleaded guilty, stating at the hearing that "he could not remember anything about the accident and believed that he might have fallen asleep while driving because he had not slept the previous night." (*Id.* at 1147.) The court imposed a prison sentence of ten years, with a four-year minimum. Gardner was apparently wrong about having caused the collision. What he did not know was that his front tire had blown out and that the tire failure, rather than an act on his part, had caused his car to swerve into oncoming traffic.

A witness in a car following Gardner's car at the time of the accident gave a written statement to the Idaho State Police that "when the blue car [Gardner's vehicle] was about ten feet in front of the truck I believe the driver's front tire blew. The whole [*sic*] jumped into the oncoming lane like it was on rails." (*Id.*) In a deposition in a subsequent civil case, "the witness explained that he observed the left front tire blowing out. He saw a puff of dust and rock chunks that appeared to have been caused by the tire blowing, then the car immediately jerked to the left." (*Id.*) The Idaho Court of Appeals applied the *Brady* disclosure duty to guilty pleas, found that the prosecution's failure to disclose the witness statement violated this duty, and vacated Gardner's guilty plea.

The *Gardner* case shows a defendant who mistakenly thought he had done something that caused another person's death. He did not have adequate knowledge to establish facts that determined his liability. Without disclosure of the witness statement, Gardner would have been wrongly convicted and would have served a significant sentence of at least four years. *Brady* disclosure here remedied a wrongful homicide conviction based on an erroneous guilty plea and prevented significant wrongful imprisonment.

Carroll v. State, 474 S.E.2d 737 (Ga. Ct. App. 1996), provides another example of a defendant who pleaded guilty when she did not know facts crucial to determining her criminal liability. As in *Gardner*, the case involved a homicide charge arising from an automobile wreck. The defendant was the 19-year-old driver of a car in which two adults and a toddler were passengers. During a heavy rainstorm, Carroll lost control of the car, which left the road, turned over, and ejected a passenger, who died. Neither alcohol nor drugs were involved.

The officer who investigated the accident scene had yet to complete a class in accident reconstruction. Despite lack of qualifications, he concluded in a written "information sheet" and in testimony at a preliminary hearing that the defendant's speed was 70 mph in a 35-mph zone and that the condition of the road and its shoulder "had no impact on the accident." Without independent knowledge of her exact speed, the road conditions, and what caused her to lose control of the car, Carroll pleaded guilty to serious felony charges in reliance on the officer's "expert" conclusions.

The investigating officer's conclusions about Carroll's speed and the role of road conditions turned out not to be supported by the evidence at the scene of the wreck. An experienced accident reconstruction expert—the instructor teaching the accident reconstruction course in which the investigating officer was enrolled—reviewed the investigating officer's work. Days before the defendant pleaded guilty, the experienced examiner concluded that it was not possible to calculate the speed of Carroll's car based on the data the investigating officer had collected and that, in his view, the condition of the road had played a role in what he viewed as an accident. In *Carroll*, as in *Gardner*, a defendant erroneously pleaded guilty because she did not know facts critical to determining her criminal liability. The Georgia Court of Appeals reversed Carroll's conviction and allowed her to withdraw her guilty plea.

Both *Gardner* and *Carroll* illustrate that there are situations in which disclosure of *Brady* material in the guilty plea context may be just as crucial to an accurate determination of criminal liability as in the trial context.

Sincerity

Lack of sincerity on a defendant's part in pleading guilty is likely a more pervasive source of inaccuracy in guilty pleas than lack of knowledge. Rather than pleading guilty because they wrongly but sincerely think they are guilty, as in *Gardner* and *Carroll*, defendants may falsely condemn themselves even though they know they are not guilty. Several Innocence Project cases have revealed such false condemnation in guilty pleas. In one case, Christopher Ochoa not only falsely condemned himself of rape and murder in an erroneous guilty plea, but also testified falsely against an innocent alleged accomplice.

Concern about sincerity in cases involving disclosure of exculpatory evidence arises from the incentives influencing both prosecutors and defendants in plea negotiations. Cases in which *Brady* material exists are particularly prone to creating incentives that encourage false self-condemnation.

The most likely response by a prosecutor who discovers *Brady* material is to dismiss the case for legal, ethical, and strategic reasons.

If the prosecutor does not dismiss, the next most likely response is to attempt to resolve the case through a guilty plea, especially if no obligation to disclose exculpatory information applies in the guilty plea context. If the prosecutor chooses to negotiate a guilty plea in a case in which *Brady* material exists, the prosecutor has an incentive to offer a large sentence differential, which in turn creates a powerful incentive for an innocent defendant to plead guilty.

Reconsider the robbery hypothetical we presented at the beginning of this chapter. The prosecution's case is based entirely on the testimony of the robbery victim, who identified the defendant from police photographs of persons with a record of similar violent crime. With only the victim's testimony to rely on, the prosecutor is unsure about obtaining a conviction at trial. Prior to trial, the victim is uncertain of her identification of the defendant. Assume that the prosecutor then offers the defendant a guilty plea limiting his sentencing exposure to five years, a significant concession in light of the defendant's substantial prior record and the fact that the charged offense carries a maximum penalty of 15 years' incarceration. On the eve of trial, the defendant indicates willingness to plead guilty if the prosecutor limits the sentence to one year. Is the prosecutor free to accept a guilty plea without disclosing the victim's statement of uncertainty about the identification?

In this scenario, exculpatory information weakening the prosecutor's case creates an incentive for the prosecutor to offer a very large discount on the potential sentence, from 15 years to one year. This sentence differential in turn creates a powerful incentive for false self-condemnation by the defendant. In sum, we should expect prosecutors if they do not dismiss to divert cases with *Brady* information from the trial to the guilty plea arena and to offer the sort of sentence differentials that undermine confidence in a defendant's admission of guilt.

State v. Johnson, 544 So. 2d 767 (La. Ct. App. 1989), strongly suggests that the defendant in that case pleaded guilty to a crime he did not commit and that failure to disclose exculpatory information contributed to that wrongful guilty plea. Johnson was charged with selling illegal drugs on two different days. The undercover officer testified that there was no doubt in her mind that the same person sold her drugs on both days and that Johnson was that individual. (*Id.* at 771.) During the trial, the defendant pleaded guilty to one of the drug offenses in return for dismissal of the other charge and an agreement not to bring perjury charges against him, his mother, or his fiancée. He received a sentence of six years at hard labor.

But state records revealed that Johnson was in state custody at the time of one of the offenses and thus could not have committed it. And the undercover officer's certainty that the same man committed both crimes indicated that Johnson had not committed the other offense. The Louisiana court set aside the guilty plea, conviction, and sentence. The facts in *Johnson* suggest that powerful incentives induced the defendant to falsely condemn himself. In addition to avoiding conviction on one of the charges, he also avoided perjury charges against himself, his mother, and his fiancée.

Brady *Disclosure as a Remedy*

Prosecutorial disclosure of exculpatory information in the guilty plea context would help remedy both lack of knowledge and lack of sincerity undermining the accuracy of guilty pleas. It would in some cases reveal and remedy a defendant's lack of knowledge about a critical element and in other cases provide a check on high sentence differentials driven by the existence of exculpatory information undermining the sincerity of a defendant pleading guilty.

Such a prosecutorial disclosure duty might be imposed by recognizing that the constitutional duty created by *Brady v. Maryland* extends to the guilty plea context or by legislative action through a statute or criminal procedure rule, such as amendment of Federal Rule of Criminal Procedure 11. Another way to create such a duty would be for ethics authorities either to interpret ABA Model Rule 3.8's "timely disclosure" obligation to attach prior to the acceptance of a guilty plea or to redraft Model Rule 3.8 to clearly impose such a disclosure duty.

Current Law

Current law on whether prosecutors must disclose exculpatory information in the guilty plea context is in a troubled and confused state. Two decades ago, the issue of whether *Brady v. Maryland*'s prosecutorial duty to disclose exculpatory evidence applies to guilty pleas had just begun to attract the attention of practitioners, judges, and commentators. Few courts, for example, had addressed the issue, and the courts that had addressed it had come to different conclusions.

By 2002, when a case dealing with *Brady* and guilty pleas first came before the U.S. Supreme Court, that situation had changed. By then a good number of federal and state cases had confronted the issue. The majority recognized that prosecutors do have a duty to disclose *Brady* material prior to a guilty plea, whereas some courts held that *Brady* does not apply in the guilty plea context.

In the past two decades, the academic literature has also given greater attention to *Brady* and guilty pleas. The first article we can find discussing *Brady* and guilty pleas was published in 1981. In the intervening 27 years, several professors and practitioners, along with a number of student authors, have written on the issue. As with judges, the overwhelming majority of commentators support requiring *Brady* disclosure prior to guilty pleas.

United States v. Ruiz

In 2002, the Supreme Court finally addressed *Brady* in the guilty plea context. In *United States v. Ruiz*, 536 U.S. 622 (2002), the Court severely restricted, and left open the possibility of entirely rejecting, application of *Brady* to guilty pleas. Though the scope of the *Ruiz* decision is ambiguous, there is little question that the case marks a significant restriction of *Brady* rights in the guilty plea context and runs counter to the trend in lower federal and state courts prior to *Ruiz*.

The context in which *Ruiz* arose is critical to evaluating the Supreme Court's decision in the case. During the 1990s, lower federal courts showed a strong trend toward applying *Brady* to guilty pleas. In a 1995 case, *Sanchez v. United States*, 50 F.3d 1448 (9th Cir. 1995), the Ninth Circuit joined this trend.

Following *Sanchez*'s holding that a defendant pleading guilty retains *Brady* rights—that such rights are not implicitly waived by entry of a guilty plea—federal prosecutors in the Southern District of California incorporated an *express* waiver of *Brady* rights in what were termed "fast-track" plea agreements. These agreements included express waiver of *Brady* as a condition of receiving lenient treatment. The express waiver, though, was not a complete waiver. The defendant waived the right to receive *Brady* material that constituted impeachment information or was relevant to an affirmative defense. But the prosecution agreed to turn over "any [known] information establishing the factual innocence of the defendant."

The defendant in *Ruiz* challenged the validity of this express *Brady* waiver as a condition to a plea agreement, and the Ninth Circuit found the express waiver unconstitutional. Despite the fact that a circuit split had developed on whether a guilty plea implicitly waives *Brady* rights, the Supreme Court did not grant certiorari in a case directly addressing that issue. Rather, the Court granted certiorari in *Ruiz*, a case presenting the more unusual issue of an express waiver of *Brady* rights prior to a guilty plea. The Supreme Court overruled the Ninth Circuit and approved the express partial waiver found in the fast-track plea agreement at issue in *Ruiz*.

The express waiver approved in *Ruiz* restricted *Brady* disclosure in two significant ways. First, it dramatically restricted the scope of *Brady* material by excluding information relevant to impeachment and affirmative defenses and including only information bearing on "factual innocence." Neither the fast-track agreement nor the Supreme Court's opinion in *Ruiz* identified the theories of relevance that fall within the phrase *factual innocence*.

The second way in which the express waiver in *Ruiz* restricted *Brady* disclosure was by raising the persuasiveness threshold required for disclosure of information bearing on *factual innocence*. Under the *Brady* rule, information must be turned over only if it is *material*. The Supreme Court's most recent iterations of the *Brady* rule define material as creating "a reasonable probability that the government's suppression [of the information] affected the outcome of the case." (*United States v. Bagley*, 473 U.S. 667, 675 (1985).) To be *Brady* material, the information "could reasonably be taken to put the whole case in such a different light as to undermine confidence in the verdict." (*Kyles v. Whitley*, 514 U.S. 419, 435 (1995).) In other words, information in the trial context must be disclosed if it is likely to create reasonable doubt in the mind of a juror.

In contrast, the disclosure obligation set forth in the plea agreement approved in *Ruiz* required disclosure only if the information *establishes* factual innocence. The phrase *establishing factual innocence* indicates that to warrant disclosure, the exculpatory information must have greater persuasive force than required by the *Brady* materiality standard. In essence, rather than create reasonable doubt about guilt, the information must prove innocence in order to mandate disclosure. The level of persuasiveness required for a particular item of favorable information to *establish* factual innocence (e.g., a preponderance standard, a clear and convincing standard, or a beyond reasonable doubt standard) was not clarified by the fast-track agreement or the Supreme Court's *Ruiz* opinion.

The *Ruiz* opinion has a number of serious flaws. First, the Court's analysis failed even to acknowledge, much less consider, the substantial body of case law from both the federal circuits and the state courts applying *Brady* in the context of guilty pleas, the primary thrust of which runs counter to the Court's analysis and conclusion. Nor did the Court acknowledge the academic commentary or address the arguments advanced therein, the primary thrust of which, again, was contrary to the *Ruiz* Court's reasoning and result. The Court's failure to acknowledge or address both prior authority and academic commentary contrary to the Court's position seriously undermines the persuasiveness of its analysis.

Second, the Court grossly overstated the burdens that disclosure of *Brady* material in the guilty plea context would impose on the government. The Court treated mandating *Brady* disclosure in the guilty plea context as the functional equivalent of open file discovery. In doing so, Justice Breyer ignored the materiality limitation on *Brady* disclosure that severely restricts what the government must produce and thus lessens the burden of producing it.

A third serious flaw in *Ruiz* is the Court's summary dismissal of any possible connection between *Brady* disclosure and wrongful conviction through guilty plea. As we discussed above, there is a highly plausible connection between failure to disclose *Brady* material and wrongful conviction through a guilty plea.

Justice Breyer, for example, devoted one short paragraph to exculpatory information relating to affirmative defenses, and a single sentence to dismissing any need for disclosure of such information. In doing so, he appeared to accept without examination a view of innocence that excludes consideration of widely accepted criminal law principles of justification and excuse. A defendant with a valid affirmative defense, in other words, appears not to qualify as *factually innocent* in Justice Breyer's view, despite the fact that substantive criminal law views such a person as not properly subject to criminal liability. The prosecutors who drafted the waiver at issue in *Ruiz* and the Supreme Court seem to view the criminal law of affirmative defenses as unworthy of enforcement in the context of a guilty plea.

Cases from lower courts, as well as academic commentary, show how disclosure of information relating to an affirmative defense can contribute to accuracy in guilty pleas. Without *Brady* disclosure in the guilty plea context, for example, a defendant may fail to raise an otherwise valid entrapment defense because the defense may not know that the person who enticed the defendant to commit the crime was an agent of the government, either an undercover law enforcement officer or a government informant. Similarly, the prosecution might have records showing that the defendant suffers from a mental illness that creates a credible basis for an insanity defense. The defendant might be incapable of or unwilling to convey this information to his or her lawyer.

Provocation provides a third example of a defense that could unwittingly be ignored in the guilty plea context without prosecutorial disclosure of *Brady* material. Some jurisdictions limit the provocation defense to certain victims. Maryland, for example, requires that "the victim was the person who provoked the rage." (*Dennis v. State*, 661 A.2d 175 (Md. Ct. Spec. App. 1995).) A defendant in a situation such as a bar fight among strangers involving multiple participants might not know after the fact whether the person killed was in fact one of the provokers. (*See State v. Lawton*, 688 A.2d 1096 (N.J. Super. Ct. App. Div. 1997).) If the prosecution has evidence unknown to the defendant showing that the victim *was* one of the provokers, such disclosure would be critical for a defendant and his or her lawyer to determine accurately the applicability of a provocation defense. Each of the affirmative defense examples just discussed illustrates that the prosecution may have information critical to ensuring a factually accurate guilty plea of which the defendant may be unaware.

Justice Breyer similarly devotes a single sentence to the possible connection between disclosure of impeachment information and the factual accuracy of guilty pleas. He concludes that the prosecution's obligation to turn over "information establishing the factual innocence of the defendant," along with Rule 11's provisions on entry of a guilty plea, "diminishes the force of Ruiz's concern that, in the absence of impeachment information, innocent individuals, accused of crimes, will plead guilty." (*Ruiz*, 536 U.S. at 631.) But when a defendant during a guilty plea hearing relies on information provided by the prosecution, rather than the defendant's independent knowledge, to establish an element of an offense or eliminate an affirmative defense, the prosecution revealing key impeachment information advances accuracy in precisely the same way it does at trial—by alerting the person relying on the information provided by the government to potential weaknesses in that information.

Implicit Waiver after Ruiz

The Court's approval in *Ruiz* of an express partial waiver of *Brady* rights as a condition to a plea bargain is clear. But what happens to *Brady* rights in the guilty plea context when the plea bargain does not contain such an express waiver? Does the very act of pleading guilty implicitly waive all or some *Brady* rights? The answer to this key question depends on how one interprets *Ruiz*.

Most commentators have argued that a guilty plea *should not*, and most lower courts have found that a guilty plea *does not*, constitute such an implicit waiver. This implicit waiver issue was not before the *Ruiz* Court, and Justice Breyer did not explicitly state a conclusion about what, if any, rights to *Brady* disclosure a defendant pleading guilty retains absent an express waiver. Also, Justice Breyer did not address the academic commentary, the arguments advanced in that commentary, or the lower court authority on implicit waiver. Nonetheless, much of the language of Justice Breyer's opinion is troublingly broad and might, unwisely in our view, be read as entirely extinguishing *Brady* rights in the context of guilty pleas.

In response to the Supreme Court's decision in *Ruiz*, the American College of Trial Lawyers proposed modifying Federal Rule of Criminal Procedure 11 to impose a duty to disclose exculpatory information in the guilty plea context. This proposal was rejected by the Federal Rules Advisory Committee. Unless such a rule is adopted, the scope of *Brady* disclosure in the guilty plea context will continue to be uncertain and contested and will depend on how lower courts and the Supreme Court interpret *Ruiz*.

Implications of Brady *Waivers*

What are the practical implications in all this? From the defense perspective, there are several lessons.

Competent and effective representation dictates that defense lawyers find out if their particular jurisdiction has resolved the issue of the constitutional right to *Brady* material in plea negotiations. As discussed above, the Court in *Ruiz* approved express waivers limited to impeachment material and affirmative defense information, but left open the question of whether a defendant retains *Brady* rights absent an express waiver. Since *Ruiz*, few jurisdictions have addressed this issue, and the pre-*Ruiz* circuit split remains. If the jurisdiction recognizes the constitutional right, the defense lawyer should inform the prosecutor and the court of the relevant law, insist on receipt of *Brady* material prior to plea negotiations, and ask the court to enforce this right. Absent an express waiver such as the type in *Ruiz*, a defense lawyer has a good faith argument that there is a constitutional right to *Brady* material in plea negotiations.

If the law is unclear, which it presently is in many jurisdictions, the defense lawyer again should request *Brady* material during plea negotiations and ask the trial court for a ruling recognizing the defendant's right to this material. The prosecutor may well provide *Brady* material in a particular case, even if not clearly constitutionally required to do so in the jurisdiction, to avoid having to brief and argue the issue. If the prosecutor hesitates to agree to provide *Brady* material during plea negotiations, that fact alone should put the defense lawyer on notice that there may be exculpatory evidence worth seeking either through independent investigation or through a court ruling. Even if the constitutional right to *Brady* material in plea negotiations is unclear, the defense lawyer can seek to make provision of such material a term of the plea agreement. If successful, the defendant then obtains a contractual right to the material.

Finally, even if the relevant jurisdiction has ruled that *Brady* does not apply to plea negotiations, the defense lawyer may nonetheless seek disclosure of exculpatory material by trying to make it a term of the plea agreement or through reliance on ethics rules such as Model Rule 3.8(d). In this regard, defense counsel should note that Comment [1] to Rule 4.1 was amended in 2002 to provide that unethical "[m]isrepresentations can also occur by . . . omissions that are the equivalent of affirmative false statements." Certain exculpatory evidence, such as the evidence in some of the cases discussed above that severely undermines the prosecution's theory of guilt or negates scientific or eyewitness evidence necessary to establish guilt, appears to us to fall within the type of omissions that are the equivalent of affirmative false statements.

What about practical and ethical implications from the prosecutor's perspective? Again, the starting point for prosecutors is to research the law and ethics rules in their jurisdictions.

If the jurisdiction imposes an obligation to reveal exculpatory material based on the *Brady* constitutional rule or a discovery rule, the prosecutor must live up to those obligations or affirmatively argue for a modification or reversal of existing law. If the law is unresolved in the particular jurisdiction, revealing *Brady* material during plea negotiations allows the prosecutor to avoid having to brief and argue the issue as well as the possibility of a constitutional violation if a court later rules that *Brady* does apply to plea negotiations. One downside of full disclosure from the prosecutor's point of view may be that in some cases prosecutors will be forced to dismiss or make more lenient offers in plea negotiations. On the other hand, revealing *Brady* material during plea negotiations may have the practical effect of preventing some defendants from pleading guilty to crimes for which they are not liable.

If the prosecutor wishes to avoid disclosure of some *Brady* material during plea negotiations, one alternative is a narrowly drafted partial *Brady* waiver of the type approved in *Ruiz*.

As noted above, the prosecutor has a clear ethical obligation in many jurisdictions to disclose exculpatory information in the government's possession in a timely fashion regardless of its materiality, admissibility, or a defense request. Ethical prosecutors, therefore, will disclose all exculpatory information in the government's possession prior to plea negotiations to insulate themselves from possible disciplinary action. Although we have found no disciplinary cases involving nondisclosure in plea negotiations stage, in *People v. Mucklow*, 35 P.3d 527 (Colo. 2000), the Colorado Supreme Court publicly censured a prosecutor for failing to disclose exculpatory information prior to a preliminary hearing, and one of the reasons North Carolina disbarred Michael Nifong was for failing to turn over exculpatory material in the pretrial stage while prosecuting members of the Duke Lacrosse Team.

Conclusion

The Court's decision in *Ruiz* approving explicit partial *Brady* waivers has left a number of unanswered questions concerning disclosure rights during plea negotiations. Because the constitutional dimension of disclosure absent an express waiver is still unsettled and its ethical aspects not widely recognized by the defense and prosecution bars, this area presents serious potential legal and ethical pitfalls. Defense lawyers and prosecutors alike should give careful consideration to the legal obligation of disclosure and their respective ethical obligations of competence and disclosure. Explicitly addressing disclosure of exculpatory material in every plea negotiation would be a positive step toward avoiding those pitfalls.

Resources for Chapter 18

Rules and Standards

MODEL RULES OF PROFESSIONAL CONDUCT 3.8, 3.8(d) and 4.1.

MODEL CODE OF PROFESSIONAL RESPONSIBILITY DISCIPLINARY RULE 7-103(B).

FEDERAL RULES OF CRIMINAL PROCEDURE 11 and 26.2.

Cases and Ethics Opinions

Brady v. Maryland, 373 U.S. 83 (1963).

Giglio v. United States, 405 U.S. 150 (1972).

United States v. Bagley, 473 U.S. 667 (1985).

State v. Johnson, 544 So. 2d 767 (La. Ct. App. 1989).
State v. Gardner, 855 P.2d 1144 (Idaho Ct. App. 1994).
Sanchez v. United States, 50 F.3d 1448 (9th Cir. 1995).
Dennis v. State, 661 A.2d 175 (Md. Ct. Spec. App. 1995).
Kyles v. Whitley, 514 U.S. 419 (1995).
Carroll v. State, 474 S.E.2d 737 (Ga. Ct. App. 1996).
State v. Lawton, 688 A.2d 1096 (N.J. Super. Ct. App. Div. 1997).
People v. Mucklow, 35 P.3d 527 (Colo. 2000).
United States v. Ruiz, 536 U.S. 622 (2002).

Articles, Reports, Books, and Other Sources

John G. Douglass, *Fatal Attraction? The Uneasy Courtship of* Brady *and Plea Bargaining*, 50 Emory L.J. 437 (2001).

Corinna Barrett Lain, *Accuracy Where It Matters*: Brady v. Maryland *in the Plea Bargaining Context*, 80 Wash. U. L. Q. 1 (2002).

Kevin C. McMunigal, *Disclosure and Accuracy in the Guilty Plea Process*, 40 Hastings L.J. 957 (1989).

Kevin C. McMunigal, *Guilty Pleas*, Brady *Disclosure, and Wrongful Convictions*, 57 Case W. Res. L. Rev. 651 (2007).

Ellen Yaroshefsky, *Ethics and Plea Bargaining—What's Discovery Got to Do with It?*, 23 Criminal Justice No. 3, 28 (Fall 2008).

CHAPTER 19

Corporate Privilege Waivers in Plea Negotiations

Recent developments—corporate scandals, the enormous amounts of money involved in those scandals, their widespread impact on stockholders and employees, and the high visibility of the prosecutions—have generated pressure for more effective, aggressive, and severe treatment of corporate crime. One focal point has been corporate attorney-client privilege. Today, federal prosecutors expect corporations to assist the government in uncovering wrongdoing within the corporation by cooperating in a number of ways.

In particular, the U.S. Department of Justice (DOJ) has adopted a policy of favoring corporate cooperation that may include waiver of corporate attorney-client privilege and work product protection as a condition of the government agreeing not to prosecute the corporation, pursuing civil penalties rather than criminal prosecution, or treating corporations favorably at sentencing if criminal prosecution is pursued.

A 2006 study by the Association of Corporate Counsel and the National Association of Criminal Defense Lawyers found that nearly 75 percent of the responding lawyers agreed that the government has developed a "culture of waiver" in which it routinely expects corporations under investigation to broadly waive privilege.

The private bar, some academic commentators, and some elected officials have criticized the practice of demanding privilege waivers. This chapter examines the ethical implications of corporate privilege waivers both for prosecutors and corporate counsel.

Corporate Attorney-Client Privilege

Corporations, like all clients, are protected by several closely related rules: attorney-client privilege, the work product doctrine, and, under modern lawyer ethics codes, client confidentiality. In determining the scope of the corporate attorney-client privilege, some jurisdictions use the "control group" test, under which only communications between the corporation's lawyer and senior managers who control the corporation's response to the lawyer's advice are privileged. Other jurisdictions use broader tests. Under one of these, communications between the corporation's lawyer and any corporate employee are privileged as long as the subject matter of the communication is within the scope of the employee's duties and made so that the corporation may obtain legal advice.

Debate about corporate waivers often focuses on noncontrol group communications made to corporation lawyers conducting an investigation at the control group's behest to determine the scope of potential wrongdoing. But DOJ guidelines on securing waivers of a corporation's privilege entail revelation of control group communications, but typically exclude communications containing legal opinions or advice by the corporation lawyers conducting the investigation.

Waivers may generate collateral damage from the corporation's point of view. An increasing number of corporations find that government investigations trigger third-party civil suits. Generally, voluntary disclosure to the government of information protected by attorney-client privilege serves as a waiver of privilege to others. Thus, corporations find it more difficult to defend shareholder suits and derivative actions once privilege is waived. Additionally, waivers and resulting disclosures may generate adverse publicity and have a negative effect on employee morale.

Competence

Competent representation of their clients by both prosecutors and defense counsel requires thorough research of the law and thorough investigation of the facts. In pursuing corporate waivers, federal prosecutors seek to increase the quantity and quality of information they have about corporate wrongdoing in order to better represent the United States. The better the information prosecutors have, the better prosecutors are able to target blameworthy corporations and employees, shield innocent corporations and employees from prosecution, and assess appropriate punishments. From a competence perspective, one might argue that prosecutors are not only ethically permitted but ethically *required* to pursue waivers in cases in which the information available to prosecutors without waiver leaves them uncertain about issues of guilt and punishment.

There are weaknesses in this argument. The prosecution is likely to have alternative means for obtaining information known by a corporation's lawyers. The privilege protects only communications, not underlying information. Prosecutors may be able to obtain underlying information through interviews with corporate employees, and through use of search warrants and grand jury subpoenas. Prosecutors can also enter into cooperation agreements with corporate employees to obtain information as well as gain the corporation's cooperation without demanding waiver.

These counterarguments are weakened if the corporation and/or its employees engage in document destruction of the sort undertaken by Enron's auditors, or if corporate employees refuse to talk to investigating agents or testify before a grand jury. In particular, if the corporation seeks to ensure that only its lawyers have a complete picture of the company's wrongdoing, it is difficult for the corporation then to complain about prosecutors demanding privilege waiver in order to fully grasp the wrongdoing prior to giving the corporation credit for cooperation.

Lawyers representing corporations also make a competence claim against waivers. The classic modern defense of attorney-client privilege, as well as the closely related ethical duty of confidentiality, is that privilege and confidentiality increase the quantity and quality of information to which lawyers have access, which in turn increases the quality of the representation those lawyers provide their clients. Corporate waivers, it is argued, reduce the quantity and quality of the information to which the corporation's lawyer has access because waivers create a disincentive for employees to reveal, and for lawyers representing corporations to seek out, information about potential wrongdoing. Ironically, waivers of corporate privilege ultimately will become worthless to the prosecution if the prospect of waiver hinders the corporation's lawyer from receiving the very information the prosecution seeks through the waiver.

But again there are weaknesses in this argument. As with the prosecution, a corporation has means other than its lawyer questioning employees to gather information. A lawyer advising a corporation has access to documents, such as checks, accounting records, and memoranda as well as e-mail, that may discuss questionable conduct. Nonlawyers working within the corporation or as outside auditors can conduct investigations that produce information that its lawyer can use to advise the corporation, using the threat of termination of employment as an incentive for full disclosure.

Both prosecutor and corporate counsel, then, can make similar competence arguments in favor of and against waivers of corporate attorney-client privilege in terms of access to information that will improve each lawyer's represention of his or her client.

Conflict of Interest

Conflict of interest is another potential ethical issue implicated by corporate waivers of attorney-client privilege. Corporate managers may confront a conflict between what is best for the corporation, which may be firing and turning over for prosecution senior managers who have engaged in criminal wrongdoing, and loyalty to colleagues as well as their own self-interest in keeping their jobs and avoiding prosecution. This tension, in turn, creates a possible conflict for corporate counsel. A lawyer representing a corporation is obligated to serve the interests of the corporation, not the interests of its employees. But senior managers typically control which lawyers the corporation retains to do its work. Thus a conflict may exist between serving the interests of the corporation and currying favor with managers who control the lawyer's future employment. Conflict of interest may also arise if the lawyer played any role in wrongdoing.

One arguable advantage of allowing the prosecution to demand waiver in certain cases is to help reveal decisions affected by conflict of interest and create an incentive for corporate lawyers to resist placing their own interests and those of senior managers over the interests of the corporation.

Brother's Keeper

Do lawyers have an ethical obligation to preserve, or at least to refrain from undermining, an opposing lawyer's relationship with and representation of the opposing lawyer's client? The anticontact rule appears to reflect such an obligation. And, as we discussed in Chapter 14, "Brother's Keeper: Must You Protect Opponent's Confidentiality?," suggestions of such an obligation may be found in ethics opinions establishing a lawyer's duty to return, without having read them, documents containing confidential information mistakenly sent to the lawyer by opposing counsel.

Just as the lawyer in the wayward document situation is compelled to act as his or her brother's keeper and refrain from undermining confidentiality between an opposing lawyer and client, the prosecutor could be viewed as having a similar obligation to refrain from undermining an opposing client's rights of confidentiality and privilege. One might argue that seeking waiver is more egregious than reading a misdirected letter or e-mail because the scope of information revealed through waiver is likely to be greater than information revealed through a wayward document. In addition, the prosecutor acts purposefully to obtain confidential and privileged information when seeking waiver, whereas a lawyer who receives a misdirected document does not.

On the other hand, the prosecution might argue that, unlike inadvertent disclosure of confidential information by a lawyer, the decision to waive privilege is consciously made by the corporate client with advice of counsel in order to gain something of value for the corporation, either freedom from prosecution or reduced liability or sanction. The threat of privilege waiver may also help keep in check lawyer conflict of interest and thereby reinforce the corporate lawyer's loyalty to the client.

A Compromise

One compromise solution to the corporate waiver issue is to allow the prosecution to demand waivers, but ensure that such waivers are used sparingly. Sparing use of waiver reduces the chances that waiver will seriously hinder corporate counsel in representing their clients. It also preserves the value of waivers for the prosecution.

The DOJ took a step toward such a compromise by issuing the "McNulty Memorandum" in December 2006. The new policy requires prosecutors to obtain high-level departmental approval before demanding a waiver. Although the new policy appears to limit the instances in which a prosecutor may demand a waiver, a report issued by former Delaware Chief Justice Norman Veasey in September 2007 demonstrated that the McNulty Memorandum had not significantly reduced the incidence of government coerced waivers. In addition, the McNulty Memorandum does nothing to end the policy that encourages waivers by rewarding companies for "unsolicited" offers to waive privilege.

In response to the mounting critique of and opposition to prosecution policies requiring waivers, the House of Representatives in November of 2007 overwhelmingly approved the Attorney-Client Privilege Protection Act of 2007. Similar legislation has been pending in the Senate since January 2007, and support for the legislation is strong. If the legislation becomes law, it will prohibit federal agencies from pressuring organizations to waive their privileges or pressuring them to take punitive action against employees as a condition for receiving cooperation credit. Facing this legislative action, the DOJ voluntarily adopted changes to its corporate guidelines in September 2008 to prohibit DOJ prosecutors from requesting corporations to disclose attorney-client privileged information or work product, or from considering whether a corporation has waived its privilege when evaluating the corporation's level of cooperation. The new guidelines will not affect state prosecutors or other federal agencies, such as the Securities and Exchange Commission or the Environmental Protection Agency, which may still continue to pressure corporations to waive attorney-client privilege. Critics argue that the DOJ policy changes do not go far enough, and Congress may still act to curtail the government's use of privilege waivers.

Resources for Chapter 19

Articles, Reports, Books, and Other Sources

Earl J. Silbert & Demme Doufekias Joannou, *Under Pressure to Catch the Crooks: The Impact of Corporate Privilege Waivers on the Adversarial System*, 43 AM. CRIM. L. REV. 1225 (2006).

Lonnie T. Brown, *Reconsidering the Corporate Attorney-Client Privilege: A Response to the Compelled-Voluntary Waiver Paradox*, 34 HOFSTRA L. REV. 897 (2006).

Michael L. Seigel, *Corporate America Fights Back: The Battle Over Waiver of the Attorney-Client Privilege*, 49 B.C. L. REV. 1 (2008).

The Association of Corporate Counsel and the National Association of Criminal Defense Lawyers, *Decline of the Attorney-Client Privilege in the Corporate Context* (2006).

Paul J. McNulty, Deputy Attorney General, *Memorandum re: Principles of Federal Prosecution of Business Organizations* (December 2006).

E. Norman Veasey, *Report to the Senate Judiciary Committee* (Sept. 13, 2007) (http://www.acc.com/public/veasey.pdf).

PART 8

Preparation for Trial

CHAPTER 20

Witness Preparation: When Does It Cross the Line?

Lawyers who practice criminal law, both prosecutors and defense counsel alike, routinely prepare witnesses for trial. James Fenimore Cooper popularized the phrase "horseshedding" to refer to the practice of lawyers rehearsing witness testimony in carriage sheds near rural courthouses in the nineteenth century. Today, some refer to witness preparation as "woodshedding" or "coaching" the witness. These colloquialisms suggest that what lawyers do in preparing witnesses is either outright unethical or at best pushes the limits of ethical conduct. But what are these ethical limits? Although the practice of witness preparation is often viewed with suspicion, the ethical and practical aspects of witness preparation are not often directly addressed.

Virtues and Vices

Why do we allow lawyers to prepare witnesses to testify? If the practice is viewed as ethically suspect, why is it not banned? A number of arguments can be made in favor of witness preparation.

Meeting with a witness prior to trial allows the lawyer to discover whether or not the witness has information relevant to the issues at trial, avoiding the time, expense, and inconvenience of having to call the witness to the stand to determine if the witness has anything of value for the fact finder. It also helps the lawyer fulfill the Rule 11 obligation to determine that there is a factual basis for the client's position. The lawyer's questions before trial may refresh the recollection of the witness and increase the amount of information available to the fact finder. Witness preparation also allows the lawyer to clarify what the witness has to say and to present the testimony in a logical sequence so that it is more readily understood at trial. Indeed, at least one court has called "[witness] preparation the mark of a good trial lawyer ... to be commended because it promotes a more efficient administration of justice and saves court time." (*State v. McCormick*, 259 S.E.2d 880, 882 (N.C. 1979).)

In addition, witness preparation gives the lawyer an opportunity to enforce the rules of evidence by instructing the witness not to mention inadmissible and possibly prejudicial information. If the lawyer, through witness preparation, learns that the witness might testify to inadmissible or prejudicial information, the lawyer can frame the questions to avoid eliciting such information.

What about the potential vices of witness preparation? Those critical of the practice argue that witness preparation allows lawyers to hide evidence unfavorable to the client and fabricate favorable evidence. Rather than increasing the quantity and quality of information available at trial, this view characterizes lawyer preparation as reducing and distorting the information available to the fact finder. Critics emphasize the malleability of witness recollection and testimony. Psychologists have demonstrated that questioning a witness can heavily influence, either purposefully or inadvertently, what the witness remembers and how he or she expresses what is recalled. Use of terms such as "coaching" and "woodshedding" to describe witness preparation tends to emphasize these negatives aspect of witness preparation.

Ethical Rules

Though there is no ethics rule specifically addressing witness preparation, there are a number of obligations that bear significantly on the practice. The obligation of competence dictates that the lawyer should thoroughly prepare the factual aspects of a case. Model Rule 1.1, for example, requires a lawyer to provide competent representation and defines competent representation as including the "thoroughness and preparation reasonably necessary for the representation." Comment [5] to Model Rule 1.1 states, "Competent handling of a particular matter includes inquiry into and analysis of the *factual* and legal *elements of the problem*, and use of methods and procedures meeting the standards of competent practitioners." (Emphasis added.) The idea that a lawyer should thoroughly investigate the facts of the case is reinforced by ethics opinions and court rules, such as Rule 11, that require factual investigation as a precursor to any filing.

One can also argue that good advocacy under the adversary system compels the lawyer to present the facts as clearly and persuasively as possible. Leading trial practice textbooks and treatises emphasize that effective direct examination depends on organizing the testimony so it is concise, understandable, and demonstrates the logical interrelationship with the party's theory of the case.

The obligation to avoid false or perjured testimony also bears on witness preparation. At the same time that the lawyer is required to investigate thoroughly and present persuasively the facts on behalf of his or her client, both the criminal law and ethical rules prohibit the lawyer from presenting false testimony. At its worst, coaching a witness may entail encouraging and assisting the witness in committing perjury. Professor Charles Wolfram has observed that "[a] lawyer who advises a witness about the law or about desired testimony before seeking the witness' own version of events comes dangerously near subornation of perjury," which may, in fact, become subornation of perjury depending on the lawyer's intent and whether or not the witness purposefully gives false testimony. (CHARLES WOLFRAM, MODERN LEGAL ETHICS § 12.4.3 (1986).)

Model Rule 3.4 states that a "lawyer shall not . . . counsel or assist a witness to testify falsely." When a lawyer crosses this line, ethical discipline usually takes the form of disbarment or suspension from the practice of law. (*See, e.g., Goodsell v. Mississippi Bar*, 667 So. 2d 7 (Miss. 1996) (imposing a six-month suspension upon a lawyer who allowed a witness to testify about a matter the lawyer knew was untrue); *In re Mitchell*, 262 S.E.2d 89 (Ga. 1979) (disbarring lawyer for encouraging witness to testify falsely); *In re Oberhellman*, 873 S.W.2d 851 (Mo. 1995) (disbarring lawyer for advising witness to testify falsely).) Criminal sanctions are also possible for witnesses who testify falsely and lawyers who encourage or assist them in doing so.

The practical and ethical task for the lawyer in witness preparation is how to comply simultaneously with these various obligations—how to investigate and present the witness's testimony thoroughly and persuasively without distorting it.

Practical Concerns

Discussions of witness preparation are often premised on the view that the lawyer's obligations to the client and the court are at odds with one another—that witness preparation that distorts a witness's testimony is good for the client, but detrimental to the court and the legal system. But there are a number of practical reasons for a lawyer to refrain from using a highly suggestive witness preparation technique. Exploration of these practical concerns reveals that avoiding distortion of witness testimony often serves the best interests of the client while at the same time protecting the legal system.

First, lawyers need to obtain accurate information about the factual strengths and weaknesses of the case in order to make strategic choices and advise a client about plea negotiations. A suggestive witness preparation technique may leave a lawyer in the dark about what a witness actually knows, reducing the amount of information the lawyer has and the quality of his or her strategic choices and advice.

Second, skeptics about witness preparation often appear to assume that witnesses are infinitely malleable, like putty in the hands of skilled trial lawyers. This may be true with some witnesses, but certainly not with all of them. By trying to shape their testimony, a lawyer runs the risk of offending and alienating potentially helpful witnesses. Heavy-handed witness preparation might even backfire by nudging the witness toward a recollection less favorable to the client than what the witness would have adopted with a more neutral inquiry.

Third, discussions of witness preparation often proceed on the unstated assumption that what the lawyer does during the process of witness preparation, because it typically goes on behind closed doors without opposing counsel present, will never be revealed. The terms "horseshedding" and "woodshedding," for example, suggest a clandestine activity not subject to review or enforcement of ethics rules.

What lawyers say to clients in preparing their testimony will normally be privileged. But what a prosecutor says to virtually any witness, and defense counsel says to any witness other than a client, is fair game for cross-examination. A skilled cross-examiner's exploration of an opposing lawyer's preparation of a witness can damage the credibility of the witness, the lawyer, and the client. Accordingly, a wise approach is to prepare the witness with the anticipation that everything said will be revealed to the fact finder. Imagine that the lawyer's exchange with the witness was being videotaped and would be played back before a jury. How would it look to the jury? How would it reflect on the lawyer's credibility, the client's credibility, and the witness's credibility?

Finally, discussions of witness preparation often fail to consider the consequences of unsuccessful witness perjury. If the lawyer does, in fact, distort the witness's testimony and that fact is revealed at trial through cross-examination or the introduction of other witnesses or documentary evidence, at the very least the credibility of the witness, the lawyer, and the client will suffer. Even if the false testimony is on a relatively minor matter, the jury may draw the inference that a witness who testifies falsely on one point is not worthy of belief on other more important points on which the witness's testimony may, in fact, be accurate and helpful to the client. There is also the possibility of criminal or other sanctions. A client who testifies falsely in a criminal case may, for example, receive a greater sentence if the sentencing judge concludes that the client testified falsely at trial.

Preparing a Witness

How can a lawyer avoid either purposefully or inadvertently distorting witness testimony, but, nonetheless, thoroughly prepare the witness? One way to think about witness preparation is to compare it to the techniques used for direct and cross-examination. Direct examination is properly pursued using nonleading, open-ended questions, whereas leading questions are appropriate during cross-examination. A suggestive witness preparation technique can be analogized to cross-examination in that it tends to suggest the witness's answers. A nonsuggestive witness preparation technique, like a good direct, does not suggest the answers. If a lawyer thinks about good witness preparation as similar to a good direct examination, it will tend to lead away from suggestive practices.

As an added benefit, the lawyer using the nonsuggestive approach will also learn about the witness's own language and word choice. Understanding the witness's way of thinking and talking about the events will help the lawyer gain a better understanding of what actually occurred and how most effectively to use the witness's testimony. Rather than a heavy hand, a light touch is often most effective in witness preparation.

Resources for Chapter 20

Rules and Standards

Model Rules of Professional Conduct 1.1 and 3.4.
Federal Rule of Civil Procedure 11.

Cases and Ethics Opinions

In re Mitchell, 262 S.E.2d 89 (Ga. 1979).
State v. McCormick, 259 S.E.2d 880 (N.C. 1979).
In re Oberhellman, 873 S.W.2d 851 (Mo. 1995).
Goodsell v. Mississippi Bar, 667 So. 2d 7 (Miss. 1996).

Articles, Reports, Books, and Other Sources

Richard C. Wydick, *The Ethics of Witness Coaching*, 17 CARDOZO L. REV. 1 (1995).

Bennett L. Gershman, *Effective Screening for Truth Telling: Is It Possible? Witness Coaching by Prosecutors*, 23 CARDOZO L. REV. 829 (2002).

CHARLES WOLFRAM, MODERN LEGAL ETHICS § 12.4.3 (1986).

CHAPTER 21

The Alternative Perpetrator Strategy

A California jury convicted David Westerfield of kidnapping and murdering seven-year-old Danielle van Dam. The Westerfield trial rekindled debate on defense lawyers defending their clients by suggesting or arguing that another person committed the crime.

The physical evidence against Westerfield was strong. Police found Danielle's fingerprints and hair inside Westerfield's home and the RV he took into the desert the weekend she disappeared. Her blood was discovered on a jacket Westerfield brought to the dry cleaner on the Monday morning after her disappearance.

The defense strategy at trial centered on suggesting that someone other than Westerfield might have kidnapped and killed Danielle. Westerfield's lawyers focused on the lifestyle of Danielle's parents, alleged "sexual swingers." According to news reports, there was testimony that the night Danielle disappeared her mother had smoked marijuana and gone out drinking and "dirty dancing" with friends and that she returned home with some of those friends. There was also testimony that the van Dams often let strangers come into their home.

The *San Diego Union-Tribune,* quoting unnamed sources, reported that Westerfield's lawyers offered early in the case to have Westerfield tell the police where to find Danielle's body if the prosecutors would not seek the death penalty. The public reacted to the story with anger and outrage. Some news commentators accused the defense lawyers of attempting intentionally to mislead the jury while knowing that their client had committed the crime. Bill O'Reilly, host of *The O'Reilly Factor,* filed an ethics complaint against Westerfield's lawyers for allegedly fabricating stories in court.

The Westerfield case raised the issue of how far a defense lawyer may go in providing a zealous and ethical defense to a client through the use of blame shifting. This chapter reviews the ethical and evidentiary rules that bear on defense use of an alternative perpetrator strategy and explores a defense lawyer's conduct in two contexts—when the defense lawyer does not know if the defendant committed the charged offense and when the lawyer does know the defendant committed the offense.

"Plan B"

Defense lawyers often focus at trial on the sufficiency of the government's proof that the defendant did the act required by the charged crime. One method of doing this is the alternative perpetrator strategy, colloquially referred to as SODDI ("some other dude did it") or simply "Plan B." Whatever the label, the strategy centers on demonstrating the insufficiency of the government's evidence by suggesting that the evidence does not eliminate the possibility that someone other than the defendant committed the crime. In addition to the Westerfield case, other well-known examples of the alternative perpetrator strategy were the efforts to shift blame to drug dealers in the O.J. Simpson case and to an unknown "Middle-Eastern looking man" in the Timothy McVeigh case. The television series *The Practice* popularized the label "Plan B" for the alternative perpetrator strategy in several fictional story lines. In each instance of Plan B, both real and fictional, the defense lawyer tries to answer the common jury question "If not the defendant, then who?"

Plan B comes in two versions, "soft" and "hard." In both, Plan B is calculated to raise doubts about the prosecution's evidence by providing the defense with the basis to argue "what ifs" such as "What if the police had continued investigating possible suspects?" or "What if the police had tracked down all the people who had access to the victim's home the night she disappeared?" In the "soft" version, the defense does not identify a specific alternative perpetrator. In the "hard" version, the defense lawyer identifies a specific alternative perpetrator. In both versions, demonstrating that someone else had the opportunity and/or motive to commit the crime strengthens the defense argument that the prosecution has failed to prove its case against the defendant beyond a reasonable doubt. In short, this strategy takes the position that if the government's evidence fails to eliminate a reasonable possibility of an alternative perpetrator, then it necessarily fails to eliminate reasonable doubt and the defendant should be acquitted.

To Use or Not to Use Plan B

The television show *The Practice* regularly portrayed the use of Plan B as, at best, morally questionable and, at worst, morally corrupt. Some lawyers share this popular view of Plan B. Ironically, though, lawyers and nonlawyers alike express a widely shared admiration for Atticus Finch, the hero of *To Kill a Mockingbird*, who used Plan B to defend an African-American defendant charged with raping a white woman in a small, segregated Southern town. Through relentless cross-examination of the complaining witness, Atticus attempted to prove that her father, rather than the defendant, had beaten her and that the charge of rape was racially motivated and fabricated to cover up the father's abuse. In this fictional context, in which Atticus believed that the charges against his client were unfounded, Plan B, even in its hard version, appears not only as an ethical but also a courageous act that has inspired generations of students to choose a career in law. Legal scholars have pointed to Atticus Finch as a model, ethical lawyer.

Would Atticus's use of Plan B have been ethical if his client had admitted committing the crime with which he was charged? The criminal justice system relies on defense lawyers to represent their clients regardless of guilt or innocence. Our law of criminal procedure requires that every criminal defendant be presumed innocent unless and until the government proves each of the elements of an offense beyond a reasonable doubt. A primary reason for requiring lawyers to defend clients regardless of factual guilt is to ensure that these rules are enforced. The Plan B strategy aims at testing the sufficiency of the government's evidence and thus enforcing the legal requirement of proof beyond reasonable doubt. Because the requirement of proof beyond reasonable doubt applies to both guilty and innocent clients alike, the standard legal ethics view is that the use of Plan B is appropriate regardless of the client's guilt.

Critiques of Plan B

There are two primary criticisms of the alternative perpetrator strategy. One is that it promotes falsity and inaccuracy. This criticism is aimed at both the soft and hard versions of Plan B. A second criticism is that the strategy is unfair to third persons—in particular those specifically targeted as possible alternative perpetrators—who are innocent. This second criticism is aimed primarily at the hard version of Plan B. The specific accusations entailed in the hard version of the alternative perpetrator strategy may cause those accused as alternative perpetrators great emotional distress, disrupt relationships with family and friends, and damage reputations in a way those accused may never be able to repair.

Falsity

Ethics rules prohibit a lawyer from introducing false evidence or assisting a client in a criminal or fraudulent act. For example, Model Rule 3.3 states that "[a] lawyer shall not knowingly . . . make a false statement of fact or law to a tribunal or . . . offer evidence that the lawyer knows to be false." The ABA Defense Function Standards take a similar position on using false evidence. Model Rule 8.4(c) states that it is professional misconduct for a lawyer to "engage in conduct involving dishonesty, fraud, deceit or misrepresentation." In addition, Model Rule 1.2 states that "[a] lawyer shall not counsel a client to engage, or assist a client, in conduct that the lawyer knows is criminal or fraudulent." Does Plan B involve the use of false evidence or fraud?

Neither the Model Rules nor the ABA Defense Function Standards specifically address Plan B. But they do require a lawyer to question the sufficiency of the government's evidence even if the lawyer knows that the client has committed the offense. For example, Standard 4-7.6(b) specifically provides that "[d]efense counsel's belief or knowledge that the witness is telling the truth does not preclude cross-examination."

Two viewpoints about the proper focal point of a trial frequently compete in both public and scholarly debate about the criminal justice system and the ethics of defense counsel. One is that criminal trials are primarily about finding the truth, an accurate account of what happened in the past. Many of the critics of the lawyers in the Westerfield case implicitly adopted this viewpoint.

The second viewpoint is that trials are not primarily about truth, but about assessing the quality of the government's proof about what happened in the past. Lawyers tend to adopt this second viewpoint. Our law of criminal procedure also adopts this second viewpoint by emphasizing that if the evidence is not sufficient to prove guilt beyond a reasonable doubt, a defendant must go free even if he or she is, in fact, guilty. For example, the instructions and verdict forms used in criminal cases pose the critical question for the jury to answer not as whether or not the defendant is guilty, but whether the government has *proven* the defendant guilty beyond reasonable doubt.

From the first viewpoint, focused on truth, lawyers using Plan B when they know their client is guilty are trying to mislead the jury into drawing a false or inaccurate conclusion about what actually happened in the past. From the second viewpoint, focused on sufficiency of evidence, those lawyers are trying to lead the jury to an accurate conclusion about the strength of the evidence the government presented at trial.

Fairness

The second critique of Plan B—that it is unfair to cast an innocent person in the role of the potential alternative perpetrator—is harder to refute than the falsity critique. In soft Plan B, a defense lawyer focuses on the possibility of some unidentified alternative perpetrator. Consequently, there is no harm to any specific third person. In hard Plan B, however, the defense lawyer does identify an alternative perpetrator. In those situations, the third party may suffer irreparable harm.

In the hard version of Plan B, whether the defense lawyer believes that the suggested alternative perpetrator is actually culpable becomes an important factor in assessing the fairness critique. For example, Atticus Finch's belief that the father was the culpable perpetrator justifies the use of Plan B even though Atticus shifted blame specifically to the father and implicitly accused the victim of perjury. If the alternative perpetrator, such as the father in *To Kill a Mockingbird*, is in fact guilty, then he deserves the harm that comes from exposing his guilt. Similarly, if the victim was committing perjury, she deserves whatever harm flows from having her perjury exposed. But, if Atticus knew that his client was guilty, shifting blame to an innocent father and impugning the honesty of a truthful victim would have caused them damage neither deserved. Is a lawyer harming innocent people in this way justifiable?

Naming a specific alternative perpetrator may strengthen an insufficiency of evidence argument by providing the jury with a concrete illustration of the weakness of the prosecution's evidence. In essence, the possible harm to innocent third parties is justified by the importance of protecting innocent defendants by enforcing the burden of proof in all criminal cases. This tolerance for harm to innocent third parties reflects the high value placed on permitting a defense lawyer to urge the jury to judge rigorously the sufficiency of the evidence.

A lawyer's use of a hard Plan B is subject to some ethical constraints. For example, Model Rule 3.4(e) states that a lawyer in trial may not "allude to any matter that the lawyer does not reasonably believe is relevant or that will not be supported by admissible evidence." In addition, Model Rule 4.4(a) states that "[i]n representing a client, a lawyer shall not use means that have no substantial purpose other than to embarrass, delay, or burden a third person."

According to ABA Defense Function Standard 4-7.6, direct and cross-examination must "be conducted fairly, objectively, and with due regard for the dignity and legitimate privacy of the witness, and without seeking to intimidate or humiliate the witness unnecessarily." Standard 4-7.6 further provides that "[d]efense counsel should not ask a question which implies the existence of a factual predicate for which a good faith belief is lacking." Thus, a lawyer using a hard Plan B must reasonably believe the strategy will be supported by admissible evidence, believe the Plan B strategy serves a substantial purpose, conduct the examination without intimidating or humiliating the witness unnecessarily, and must not ask questions lacking a good faith factual basis.

But the foregoing limitations on a hard Plan B are tempered by Model Rule 3.1's provision that a "lawyer for the defendant in a criminal proceeding . . . may nevertheless so defend the proceeding as to require that every element of the case be established." ABA Defense Function Standard 4-7.7 goes further by expressly permitting defense counsel "in closing argument to the jury, [to] argue all reasonable inferences from the evidence in the record." Thus, these ethics rules permit the use of a hard Plan B that enables the defense lawyer to put the prosecution's evidence to the test and permit the lawyer to argue all reasonable inferences from the evidence even if the lawyer knows the client is guilty.

Strategic self-interest may also constrain the use of a hard Plan B. For example, a jury might react negatively to an attempt to shift blame to a sympathetic alternative perpetrator. In addition, the use of Plan B is governed by rules of evidence that provide some measure of protection for third persons.

Evidentiary Limits on Plan B

Evidence law in a majority of jurisdictions prohibits introducing evidence of an alternative perpetrator unless there is a "direct connection" between the alternative perpetrator and the crime.

Defense counsel must produce either "some evidence" or "substantial evidence," depending on the state, linking the alternative perpetrator to the crime. In some states, the direct connection hurdle is quite high and requires that the evidence "clearly implicate someone besides the accused as the guilty person." (*State v. Clark*, 859 S.W.2d 782, 788 (Mo. App. 1993); *see also Romano v. State*, 847 P.2d 368, 381 (Okla. Crim. App. 1993) (requiring evidence "clearly to point to another, rather than the accused").) The direct connection requirement appears to be based on avoiding harm to third parties as well as concerns about jury confusion and undue consumption of time.

In *People v. Green*, 609 P.2d 468, 480 (Cal. 1980), the California Supreme Court explained: "It is settled . . . that evidence that a third person had a motive to commit the crime with which the defendant is charged is inadmissible if it simply affords a possible ground of suspicion against such person; rather, it must be coupled with substantial evidence tending to directly connect that person with the actual commission of the offense." The Georgia Supreme Court in *Klinect v. State*, 501 S.E.2d 810, 814 (Ga. 1998), held that "the proffered evidence must raise a reasonable inference of the defendant's innocence, and must directly connect the other person with the *corpus delicti*, or show that the other person has recently committed a crime of the same or similar nature."

The United States Supreme Court has ruled, however, that there are limits to the hurdles that may be imposed on a defendant's use of alternative perpetrator evidence. In *Holmes v. South Carolina*, 547 U.S. 319 (2006), the Court addressed a South Carolina evidence rule that prohibited a defendant from introducing evidence of an alternative perpetrator whenever a trial court concluded that there was "strong evidence" of the defendant's guilt. In a unanimous decision, the Court held that by focusing solely on the strength of the prosecutor's case and not including the probative value of defense evidence of third-party guilt, South Carolina's approach was arbitrary and violated "a criminal defendant's right to have 'a meaningful opportunity to present a complete defense.'" (*Id.* at 331 (*quoting Crane v. Kentucky*, 476 U.S. 683, 690 (1986)).) In reaching its decision, the Court in dicta approved excluding alternative perpetrator evidence when it does not sufficiently connect the alleged perpetrator to the crime. (*See Holmes*, 547 U.S. at 327.)

Rigorous direct connection limitations on Plan B are at odds with the ethics rules' permissive attitude toward Plan B. Such direct connection rules also require of defense counsel investigation of possible alternative perpetrators that may exceed the limited resources of many defense lawyers.

Some commentators have argued that high direct connection hurdles undermine the burden of proof, disrupt the balance of the adversarial system, and may even impair a defendant's Sixth Amendment jury trial right. As Professor Wigmore stated:

> [I]f the evidence is in truth calculated to cause the jury to doubt, the court should not attempt to decide for the jury that this doubt is purely speculative and fantastic, but should afford the accused every opportunity to create that doubt. A contrary rule is unfair to a really innocent defendant. (1A WIGMORE, EVIDENCE § 139, at 1724 (Tillers Rev. 1983).)

Conclusion

The Plan B strategy has its virtues and its vices. Television portrayals of the alternative perpetrator strategy have found dramatic value in the tension between these virtues and vices. Lawyers using the alternative perpetrator strategy advance a worthwhile goal—making the government produce sufficient evidence before convicting someone of a crime. In pursuing Plan B, lawyers may shield a guilty client from conviction but harm innocent third parties. Such negative consequences of Plan B are obvious, vivid, and concrete, whereas the good it produces is often abstract and all but invisible to a public that sees trials as primarily about accurately determining historical truth rather than assessing the adequacy of evidence. It is little wonder that use of Plan B in the Westerfeld trial sparked anger and outrage. There is little doubt that it will continue to do so.

Resources for Chapter 21

Rules and Standards

MODEL RULES OF PROFESSIONAL CONDUCT 1.2, 3.1, 3.3, 3.4(e), 4.4(a), and 8.4(c).

ABA CRIMINAL JUSTICE STANDARDS FOR THE DEFENSE FUNCTION, Standards 4-7.6 and 4-7.7.

Cases and Ethics Opinions

People v. Green, 609 P.2d 468 (Cal. 1980).

Crane v. Kentucky, 476 U.S. 683 (1986).

Romano v. State, 847 P.2d 368 (Okla. Crim. App. 1993).

State v. Clark, 859 S.W.2d 782 (Mo. App. 1993).
Klinect v. State, 501 S.E.2d 810 (Ga. 1998).
Holmes v. South Carolina, 547 U.S. 319 (2006).

Articles, Reports, Books, and Other Sources

Ellen Yankiver Suni, *Who Stole the Cookie from the Cookie Jar?: The Law and Ethics of Shifting Blame in Criminal Cases*, 68 FORDHAM L. REV. 1643 (2000).
1A WIGMORE, EVIDENCE § 139, at 1724 (Tillers Rev. 1983).

PART 9

Litigation Ethics

CHAPTER 22

Prosecutors Pursuing Inconsistent Prosecutions

Is it permissible for prosecutors to pursue factually inconsistent prosecutions in successive trials seeking to convict different defendants of a crime that only one could have committed? Should the prosecutor's duty to protect the innocent in such cases outweigh the duty to convict the guilty? If so, does pursuing inconsistent prosecutions violate the duty to protect the innocent? Or does arguing inconsistent positions better enforce the rights of the public by maximizing the possibility that the guilty will be punished? Courts and legal commentators have explored these questions, which have arisen in a number of cases.

Initially, one might wonder how one jury could conclude that there is proof beyond reasonable doubt that A committed a crime that only one person could have committed when there exists enough evidence for a second jury to conclude that B committed the same crime. It would seem that the evidence against B would create reasonable doubt regarding A, and that the evidence against A would create reasonable doubt regarding B. But courts routinely exclude from criminal trials evidence that a person other than the defendant committed a crime. This exclusion of alternate perpetrator evidence is what allows prosecutors to make the sort of factually inconsistent arguments necessary to pursue inconsistent prosecutions as addressed in this chapter.

Advancing Inconsistent Theories of Prosecution

Inconsistent factual arguments by prosecutors can be made in a variety of scenarios. Consider the following example, loosely based on *Jacobs v. Scott*, 31 F.3d 1319 (5th Cir. 1994). Assume there is evidence pointing to two different persons, A and B, as the perpetrator of a crime. Each denies responsibility. In A's trial, A claims to have witnessed B commit the crime. The prosecutor urges the jury to reject A's testimony, and the jury returns a verdict against A. In a subsequent trial, against B, the prosecution calls A as the key witness who testifies again that B was the sole perpetrator. The prosecutor asks the jury to return a verdict against B based on A's testimony, and the jury convicts B.

In the first trial, the prosecutor attacks and discredits A's testimony in order to convict A. In the second trial, the prosecutor endorses A's testimony in order to convict B. In this example, if the jury convicts both A and B, it is certain that an innocent person will be convicted, though the prosecutor may not know which of the defendants is innocent.

Here is another example, loosely based on *Nichols v. Collins*, 802 F. Supp. 66 (S.D. Tex. 1992), *rev'd sub nom. Nichols v. Scott*, 69 F.3d 1255 (5th Cir. 1995). Assume two robbers exchange gunfire with police as they attempt to escape the robbery scene. A bullet from one robber's gun kills an innocent victim, but the police are unable to determine which robber fired the fatal shot. Assume that both robbers are guilty of felony murder, but that under the applicable law only the robber who fired the fatal shot qualifies for the death penalty. The prosecutor, though, charges both defendants with capital murder on the basis of each having fired the fatal shot. The prosecutor knows that it is a factual impossibility for both defendants to have fired the fatal shot, but in separate trials the prosecutor introduces and relies on evidence that points to each defendant as the responsible shooter. In this example, both defendants have committed robbery and felony murder, but only one qualifies for the death penalty. Thus, if both are sentenced to death, one will receive a punishment he does not legally deserve.

The 2003 trials of John Allen Muhammad and Lee Boyd Malvo for sniper killings in the D.C. metropolitan area represent a third type of factually inconsistent prosecution. In the first case, the prosecutors' theory was that the 42-year-old Muhammad brainwashed the 17-year-old Malvo, rendering Malvo an irresponsible agent of Muhammad. At the same time the prosecutor from one Virginia county was delivering his closing argument in the Muhammad case, the prosecutor from another Virginia county in Malvo's case maintained that Malvo was an equally responsible participant in the shootings. In his closing argument in Malvo's case, the prosecutor argued that the jury should reject the defense theory that

Malvo was not responsible for his acts because he had been brainwashed by Muhammad. The prosecution's theories regarding Malvo's responsibility in the two different trials directly contradicted one another. Should the prosecutors have been allowed to make such inconsistent arguments? Should it matter that the prosecutors, both representing the state of Virginia, were from separate offices in different counties?

A Prosecutor's Options

The prosecutor usually has three options when there is evidence pointing to two different defendants and only factually inconsistent arguments could convict both. First, the prosecutor can acknowledge the uncertainty of the evidence and decide not to pursue charges against either defendant that require the use of inconsistent factual arguments.

Second, the prosecutor may select the defendant most likely to have committed the offense and pursue a case only against that defendant. In the first example, this may result in pursuing charges only against A. In the other two examples, the prosecutor would pursue the death penalty against only one of the defendants.

Finally, the prosecutor could choose to pursue inconsistent prosecutions against both defendants. As mentioned previously, this means in the first example that an innocent person might be convicted. In the felony murder hypothetical, if both are convicted, it means that one defendant will receive an unwarranted punishment.

Why Do Prosecutors Do It?

Doesn't fear of convicting an innocent person dissuade prosecutors from prosecuting two different defendants for the same crime? It doubtless does in many situations. But federal and state cases reveal that there have been quite a few prosecutors willing to pursue such charges.

What motivates some prosecutors to proceed against two defendants despite the obvious risk of convicting an innocent person? One explanation may be that, though only one person may have committed the crime, the prosecutor views both defendants as morally bad actors, such as the two robbers in the felony murder example. The prosecutor may also conclude that, although only one defendant committed the crime, both may be able to provide evidence about who committed the crime. The prosecutor thus may be motivated to initiate charges against both in order to force cooperation from both defendants. Another reason for such dual prosecutions may be public pressure to make sure that the guilty defendant does not escape punishment.

Prosecutors may also view themselves as simply advocates in an adversarial system who are not responsible for the factual accuracy of the convictions their prosecutions bring about. They may think it their duty only to marshal the evidence and make the arguments, leaving the task of sorting out guilt and innocence solely to juries.

Model Rule of Professional Conduct 3.8 outlines the special ethical responsibilities of a prosecutor and states in subsection (a) that the prosecutor shall "refrain from prosecuting a charge that the prosecutor knows is not supported by probable cause." Prosecutors advancing inconsistent arguments may feel that if a judge at a preliminary hearing or a grand jury has found probable cause, they are relieved of any further responsibility regarding the guilt or innocence of the accused.

The probable cause standard is a low one that the Supreme Court has stated is not subject to any precise definition and is essentially equivalent to a "reasonable ground for belief of guilt." (*Brinegar v. United States*, 338 U.S. 160, 175 (1949).) Cases involving factually inconsistent prosecutorial theories and factual arguments, though, do bring into question whether the prosecutor can possibly claim to know that a case is supported by probable cause if there exists enough evidence to convict another person of the same crime. It seems logically inescapable that the evidence against one would negate probable cause against the other. However, the probable cause determinations made by a judge at a preliminary hearing and by a grand jury in returning an indictment are usually made without considering any exculpatory evidence. And different juries may find proof beyond reasonable doubt to convict both A and B, especially if the juries are not informed that the government is pursuing factually inconsistent theories of prosecution.

The Pursuit of Inconsistent Prosecutions

Prosecutors should not pursue factually inconsistent prosecutions for several reasons. First, the prosecutor has a different set of duties than the defense lawyer. The defense lawyer has no obligation to make sure the guilty are convicted and has no duty to protect innocent persons, other than the client. The prosecutor, by contrast, has *both* a duty to convict the guilty and a duty to protect the innocent.

These dual obligations are often expressed by describing the prosecutor as both an advocate and a minister of justice. (*See* Model Rules of Prof'l Conduct R. 3.8 cmt. 1.) In pursuing factually inconsistent arguments, prosecutors focus solely on procedural justice and ignore any obligation to monitor the substantive injustice of convicting an innocent person.

Second, under our justice system, protection of the innocent and conviction of the guilty are not equally important. As the beyond reasonable doubt standard of proof reflects, the duty to protect the innocent is given much greater weight than the duty to convict the guilty. Justice John Marshall Harlan stated, it is a "fundamental value determination of our society that it is far worse to convict an innocent man than to let a guilty man go free." (*In re Winship*, 397 U.S. 358, 372 (1970) (Harlan, J., concurring).) The greater comparative importance of protecting the innocent as opposed to convicting the guilty is reflected in common prosecutorial practices. Prosecutors, for example, routinely and appropriately exercise discretion *not* to prosecute some people known to be guilty because the purposes of punishment or the cost of prosecution do not warrant prosecution. Here, the duty to convict the guilty is secondary to other policy and pragmatic considerations. By contrast, the prosecutor has no discretion to prosecute people known to be innocent. This duty is not subordinated to other considerations.

Finally, public respect and trust in our criminal justice system will suffer if factually inconsistent charges are pursued that result in an innocent person being convicted. Imagine, for example, how the jurors in our first example would feel about the prosecutor and the criminal justice system in which they participated if they learned about the second prosecution. Having followed the prosecutor's urging to disbelieve and convict A, they would learn that the prosecutor urged another jury to believe A and convict B, and that both A and B were convicted of a crime only one could have committed. Such jurors may well conclude that they have convicted an innocent person. And they would likely conclude that a prosecutor who, after urging them *not* to believe A, exhorted another jury to believe A is not worthy of trust or public office.

Ethical Requirements for Prosecutors

Although one might think that ethics rules other than Model Rule 3.8 (a)'s requirement of probable cause would provide clear guidance to prosecutors considering the use of inconsistent prosecutions, they do not. Model Rule 3.3 prohibits both the defense and prosecution from knowingly presenting false evidence. Model Rule 3.4 cmt. 1 bans "destruction or concealment of evidence, improperly influencing witnesses, obstructive tactics in discovery procedures and the like." But the prosecutor, in advancing factually inconsistent arguments, is neither presenting false evidence nor tampering with evidence or witnesses. Instead, the prosecutor is making a selective presentation of often circumstantial evidence and arguing to the jury that the evidence is sufficient to support convictions in each case.

The ABA Prosecution Function Standards provide no specific guidance on the prosecutor's use of factually inconsistent arguments. But commentary to Standard 3-1.1 states that the prosecutor is a "minister of justice" obliged "to protect the innocent as well as to convict the guilty, to guard the rights of the accused as well as to enforce the rights of the public." These standards articulate clearly the dual nature of the prosecutor's duties, but they do not specifically address the pursuit of factually inconsistent prosecutions.

Possible Limits on Inconsistent Prosecutions

A number of courts have expressed discomfort with the practice of prosecutors pursuing inconsistent prosecutions because, as stated above, it appears at odds with the prosecutor's role as a minister of justice. In most of these cases, courts have found other grounds for reversal, such as ineffective assistance of defense counsel or the failure of the prosecution to disclose exculpatory evidence. Some of these courts, though, have stated that the practice can violate a defendant's due process rights.

In *Thompson v. Calderon*, 120 F.3d 1045 (9th Cir. 1997) (en banc), *rev'd* 523 U.S. 538 (1998), the prosecution charged roommates Thomas Thompson and David Leitch with rape and capital murder in the death of Ginger Fleischli, Lietch's girlfriend. At the preliminary hearing, before Thompson's and Leitch's requests for separate trials were granted, the prosecution's theory was that Leitch wanted the victim dead because she was interfering with his attempts to reconcile with his ex-wife. The prosecutor used four jailhouse informants who testified that Leitch had enlisted Thompson's assistance in the murder. After the cases were severed for trial, the prosecutor at Thompson's trial used jailhouse informants who testified that Thompson had confessed that he killed the victim to prevent her from reporting that he had raped her. The prosecutor objected to testimony by defense witnesses who were called to testify about Leitch's violent disposition, threats toward the victim, and motive to kill the victim. In the trial against Leitch, the same prosecutor called the defense witnesses from the Thompson trial to establish Leitch's motive to kill the victim because Leitch thought the victim was interfering with his efforts to reconcile with his ex-wife. In closing arguments at each trial, the prosecutor argued that only the defendant on trial had any motive to kill the victim. (*See id.* at 1055–57.)

Although the Ninth Circuit reversed Thompson's capital murder conviction on ineffective assistance of counsel grounds, four judges stated that they would have reversed based on the ground that "the prosecutor's use of fundamentally inconsistent theories at his and Leitch's trials violated due process." (*Id.* at 1056.) In reaching their decision, the judges found that the prosecutor had "manipulated evidence and witnesses, argued inconsistent motives, and at Leitch's trial essentially ridiculed the theory he had used to obtain a conviction and death sentence at the Thompson trial." (*Id.* at 1057.)

Relying on several Supreme Court and Ninth Circuit decisions discussing the prosecutor's duty to administer justice and the prohibition against presenting false evidence, the four judges stated that "it is well established that when no new significant evidence comes to light a prosecutor cannot, in order to convict two defendants at separate trials, offer inconsistent theories and facts regarding the same crime." (*Id.* at 1058.) We have found, though, only one case in which a court reversed a conviction on due process grounds arising out of a prosecutor's use of inconsistent arguments. In *Smith v. Groose*, 205 F.3d 1045 (8th Cir.) *cert. denied sub nom. Gammon v. Smith*, 531 U.S. 985 (2000), the prosecution used two contradictory statements from an informant to convict two different defendants, Jon Smith and Michael Cunningham, of burglary and murder. The informant implicated Smith in his first statement to the police. Then, in a later statement, the informant recanted his first statement implicating Smith and instead implicated Cunningham. (*Id.* at 1047–48.)

At Smith's trial, the prosecutor used the first statement of the informant to impeach testimony in which he implicated Cunningham. The prosecutor successfully argued that under Missouri evidence rules the informant's prior inconsistent statement could be used as substantive evidence of Smith's guilt. After Smith's trial and conviction, the state indicted Cunningham for the murder. At Cunningham's trial, the same prosecutor relied on the second statement from the informant and his testimony, which was consistent with the informant's testimony at Smith's trial, to convict Cunningham. In reversing Smith's conviction, the court held that using inconsistent theories is a due process violation if the prosecutor presents "inherently contradictory" evidence and arguments that go to the "core of the prosecutor's cases" in separate trials against the defendants. (*Id.* at 1051–52.) The court reasoned that "what the State claimed to be true in Smith's case it rejected in Cunningham's case, and vice versa." (*Id.* at 1050.) In reversing Smith's conviction, the court stated that the "manipulation of the evidence deprived him of due process and rendered his trial fundamentally unfair. . . . The State's duty to its citizens does not allow it to pursue as many convictions as possible without regard to fairness and the search for truth." (*Id.* at 1051.)

The Supreme Court has left open the question of whether inconsistent prosecutions constitute a due process violation. In *Bradshaw v. Stumpf*, 545 U.S. 175 (2005), the Sixth Circuit granted habeas corpus relief and permitted John David Stumpf to withdraw his guilty plea, reasoning that it was not knowing, voluntary, and intelligent because of the prosecution's inconsistent factual theories concerning the identity of the triggerman in a murder. Stumpf had pled guilty to attempted aggravated murder and one count of aggravated murder with one capital specification, and in exchange the state dropped several nonmurder charges and two capital murder specifications. In entering the plea, Stumpf maintained that he aided and abetted another, Clyde Daniel Wesley, but that he, Stumpf, had not shot the victim. At the sentencing hearing, the prosecution argued that the evidence indicated that Stumpf was the actual shooter, and Stumpf received the death penalty. At Wesley's later trial, the prosecutor argued that Wesley was the triggerman. Wesley argued that the same prosecutor had taken a contrary position in Stumpf's case, and the jury sentenced Wesley to life imprisonment. Writing for a majority of the Court, Justice O'Connor noted that under Ohio law an aider and abettor to murder could receive the death penalty, so that Stumpf's plea of guilty was not affected by the government's inconsistent arguments. (*Id.* at 184.) However, the Court remanded the case to the Sixth Circuit to determine if the prosecutor's inconsistent arguments affected the sentencing. The Court reasoned that "it is at least arguable that the sentencing panel's conclusion about Stumpf's principal role in the offense was material to its sentencing determination." (*Id.* at 187.) The Court stated that it would be premature for it to resolve the sentencing claim, and that the Court "express[es] no opinion on whether the prosecutor's actions [in making inconsistent arguments] amounted to a due process violation, or whether any such violation would have been prejudicial." (*Id.*)

In addition to due process possibly curbing inconsistent arguments by prosecutors, Professor Anne Bowen Poulin has argued that courts should use three legal tools for discouraging prosecutorial inconsistency: (1) introducing the prosecutor's prior inconsistent statements as party admissions; (2) applying collateral estoppel; and (3) using judicial estoppel. (Anne Bowen Poulin, *Prosecutorial Inconsistency, Estoppel, and Due Process: Making the Prosecution Get Its Story Straight*, 89 Calif. L. Rev. 1423 (2001).)

Conclusion

Except in extreme instances, such as those in *Thompson v. Calderon* and *Smith v. Groose*, current ethics and criminal procedure rules provide a prosecutor with little guidance regarding inherently contradictory trial strategies. Because of this ambiguity, it is all the more important for prosecutors to realize the dual nature of their duties and to realize that, unlike defense lawyers, they have a responsibility to monitor and help ensure the substantive justice their prosecutions produce. Only if the prosecutor is satisfied that factually inconsistent prosecutions are not likely to convict an innocent person should the prosecutor proceed with such prosecutions.

Resources for Chapter 22

Rules and Standards

Model Rules of Professional Conduct 3.3, 3.4, and 3.8.

ABA Criminal Justice Standards for the Prosecution Function, Standard 3-1.1.

Cases and Ethics Opinions

Brinegar v. United States, 338 U.S. 160, 175 (1949).

In re Winship, 397 U.S. 358 (1970).

Jacobs v. Scott, 31 F.3d 1319 (5th Cir. 1994).

Nichols v. Collins, 802 F. Supp. 66 (S.D. Tex. 1992), *rev'd sub nom. Nichols v. Scott*, 69 F.3d 1255 (5th Cir. 1995).

Thompson v. Calderon, 120 F.3d 1045 (9th Cir. 1997) (en banc), *rev'd* 523 U.S. 538 (1998).

Smith v. Groose, 205 F.3d 1045 (8th Cir.) *cert. denied sub nom. Gammon v. Smith*, 531 U.S. 985 (2000).

Bradshaw v. Stumpf, 545 U.S. 175 (2005).

Articles, Reports, Books, and Other Sources

Barry Tarlow, *Limitations on the Prosecution's Ability to Make Inconsistent Arguments in Successive Claims*, 21 CHAMPION 40 (1997).

Anne Bowen Poulin, *Prosecutorial Inconsistency, Estoppel, and Due Process: Making the Prosecution Get Its Story Straight*, 89 CALIF. L. REV. 1423 (2001).

CHAPTER 23

"Thou Shalt Not Use Religion in Closing Argument"

The place of religion in the courts is often a hot news topic. Frequently, parties sue to remove religious symbols from courthouses around the country. Chief Justice Roy Moore fought and ultimately ignored a court order to remove a monument of the Ten Commandments from the Alabama Supreme Court rotunda. The U.S. Supreme Court refused to hear his appeal, and, in a unanimous decision, the Alabama Court of the Judiciary removed Moore from the bench for disobeying a lawful court order. If the Ten Commandments do not belong in a courthouse rotunda, do the Ten Commandments, the Bible, and other religious imagery have a place in closing arguments? Dozens of state and federal courts have considered the use of religious references and imagery in closing arguments. This chapter looks at the use of religion in closing arguments, when it constitutes misconduct, and when it leads to reversal.

The Bounds of Argument

Trial and appellate judges grant both prosecution and defense wide latitude in closing arguments. Counsel are entitled to argue the inferences the jurors should draw from and the weight jurors should give to particular items of evidence. The credibility and demeanor of witnesses are proper topics for argument in addition to rebutting the arguments of opposing counsel. Lawyers may use analogies, anecdotes, references to current events, and well-worn quotes and stories to persuade the jury about how to view the evidence in the case.

Arguments based upon the Bible and use of religious imagery, however, have raised red flags. Courts have shown particular concern when prosecutors make religious references during the sentencing phase of capital cases. Most courts view such arguments as improper and place strict limits on them in closing.

Model Rule of Professional Conduct 3.4, the primary rule dealing with argument, states that a "lawyer shall not . . . in trial, allude to any matter that the lawyer does not reasonably believe is relevant or that will not be supported by admissible evidence, assert personal knowledge of facts in issue except when testifying as a witness, or state a personal opinion as to the justness of a cause, the credibility of a witness, the culpability of a civil litigant or the guilt or innocence of an accused." The ABA's Standards for Criminal Justice echo these limits and explain in greater detail the limits on appealing to the jury with matters not supported by the evidence. Defense lawyers and prosecutors are specifically told they "should not make arguments calculated to appeal to the prejudices of the jury," and they "should refrain from arguments that would divert the jury from its duty to decide the case on the evidence." (Criminal Justice Standard 3-5.8, 4-7.7).

Although the ethics rules and the Standards for Criminal Justice define the ethical duties for defense lawyers and prosecutors in the same terms, the commentary to Criminal Justice Standard 3-5.8 states the following: "Prosecutorial conduct in argument is a matter of special concern because of the possibility that the jury will give special weight to the prosecutor's arguments, not only because of the prestige associated with the prosecutor's office but also because of the fact-finding facilities presumably available to the office." The commentary to Standard 3-5.8 recognizes that "a prosecutor must be free to present arguments with logical force and vigor," and then states "[a]s the Supreme Court has remarked, however, 'while he [the prosecutor] may strike hard blows, he is not at liberty to strike foul ones.'" (Quoting *Berger v. United States*, 295 U.S. 78, 88 (1935).) The Court in *Berger* explained the underlying rationale: "The United States Attorney is the representative . . . of a sovereignty . . . whose interest . . . in a criminal prosecution is not that it shall win a case, but that justice shall be done. . . . It is as much his duty to refrain from improper methods calculated to produce a wrongful conviction as it is to use every legitimate means to bring about a just one." (*Id.* at 88.)

Establishing the difference between "hard" and "foul" blows can be difficult, but substantial case authority provides guidance. The commentary to Criminal Justice Standard 4-7.7 notes that due to the unavailability of government appeals in most criminal cases, few courts have considered the limits of defense arguments. Nonetheless, the courts that have considered the legal and ethical boundaries of closing arguments apply the same general limitations to both prosecutors and defense counsel.

Religious References and Misconduct

Remarks calculated to evoke bias, prejudice, or passions "should never be made in a court of justice." (*People v. Simon*, 252 P. 758, 760 (Cal. App. 1927); *see also* Criminal Justice Standard 4-7.7.) Although appealing to the passions and prejudices of the jury is proscribed, the tradition of zealous advocacy in the United States, the emotional impact of crimes, and the severe consequences of conviction often tempt lawyers in criminal cases to appeal to jurors by any means possible—especially through stories jurors understand. With more than 90 percent of Americans indicating that they believe in God, parables and other religious stories can be very effective in communicating lawyers' messages to jurors, as well as in appealing to their consciences.

References to jurors' religious faith or principles, however, may prompt the jurors to ignore the controlling law and the facts of the case. "[B]y conjuring up images of religion, the remarks improperly appeal to the jury to act in ways other than as dispassionate arbiters of the facts." (*United States v. Levy-Cordero*, 67 F.3d 1002, 1008 (1st Cir. 1995).) In short, religious principles may not replace legal principles as governing conviction for a crime. Religiously charged closing arguments are not only unethical, but in some instances may violate the accused's due process right to a fair trial and serve as the grounds for reversal and a new trial.

One high-profile example of a defense lawyer using a biblical story in closing argument was in the death penalty case of Susan Smith, convicted of murdering her two young sons. Pleading for mercy during the sentencing phase, Smith's lawyer picked up the court clerk's Bible and repeated the parable of the adulterous woman, quoting "[h]e who is without sin among you, let him first cast a stone." He went on to tell the jurors, "You each have a stone, with 12 in all . . . [b]ut no stone may be thrown unless all are thrown." The jurors—five of whom listed church affiliations in their jury questionnaires—unanimously decided against the death penalty.

The prosecutor in the *Smith* case did not object to the religious reference, although it was improper. Because the prosecutor failed to object, the judge did not admonish defense counsel. However, in another death penalty case in which the defense interjected religion during the sentencing phase, the Pennsylvania Supreme Court affirmed a trial judge who sustained the prosecution's objections. (*Pennsylvania v. Daniels*, 644 A.2d 1175, 1183 (Pa. 1994).) Relying on ABA Standard for Criminal Justice 4-7.8, the *Daniels* court stated that the same rationale that prohibits the prosecutor's reliance on religious writings in support of the death penalty also prohibits the defense from relying on religious writings "to inflame the passions or prejudices of the jury, or to divert the jury from its duty to decide the case on the evidence." (*Id.*)

In another death penalty case, *Carruthers v. State*, 528 S.E.2d 217 (Ga. 2000), the prosecutor read aloud passages from the Bible, including "whoever sheds another person's blood shall have his own blood shed by man," and "[those] who take the sword shall die by the sword." (*Id.* at 222.) The prosecutor stated that these passages contain "a message that is very clear, that society must deter criminals." (*Id.*) In considering whether the prosecutor's remarks were outside the bounds of proper argument, the Georgia Supreme Court held that "[l]anguage of command and obligations from a source other than Georgia law should not be presented to the jury," and that the prosecutor's reading of the Bible as the law to be followed violated the defendant's due process rights during the sentencing phase. (*Id.*)

The courts also disapprove of the *golden rule* argument, which suggests to jurors that they place themselves in the position of the victim and decide the case accordingly. The golden rule argument is based on the biblical quote "As ye would that men should do to you, do ye also to them likewise." (6 *Luke* 31.) In an aggravated assault case, the prosecutor crossed the lines of proper argument by asking the jurors to "imagine how terrifying" it would be to have the light from a laser-sighted gun "on your chest." (*DeFreitas v. State*, 701 So. 2d 593, 601 n.7 (Fla. Dist. Ct. App. 1997).) In reversing the case, the Florida appellate court stated that "the line between the inflammatory and the dramatic is not always clear" but "as far as golden rule arguments are concerned, the lines are clear and bright, simply put they are improper. In short, they enjoy no safe harbor in the trial of a criminal case." (*Id.* at 601.)

More recently, in *State v. Ceballos*, 832 A.2d 14 (Conn. 2003), the Connecticut Supreme Court examined the use of religion in closing arguments by prosecutors, and joined "'federal and state courts [that] have universally condemned . . . religiously charged arguments as confusing, unnecessary, and inflammatory.'" (*Id.* at 29 (*citing Bennett v. Angelone*, 92 F.3d 1336, 1346 (4th Cir.), *cert. denied*, 519 U.S. 1002 (1996)).) In surveying state and federal courts, the Connecticut Supreme Court found that although a majority of jurisdictions have held that the "prosecutorial use of religious references is always improper," there is less agreement on whether "all improper religious remarks constitute harmful or reversible error." (*Ceballos*, 832 A.2d at 29–30.)

Reversible Error?

Not all religious references in closing arguments constitute reversible error. However, arguing that the jury should follow religious teachings in reaching a verdict regardless of the law, as in *Carruthers*, almost always results in reversible error. The Ninth Circuit, for example, held that a prosecutor who paraphrased biblical passages to justify the death penalty during the penalty phase of a capital trial was "improper and highly prejudicial" because "delegation of the ultimate responsibility for imposing a sentence to divine authority undermines the jury's role in the sentencing process." (*Sandoval v. Calderon*, 241 F.3d 765, 775–77 (9th Cir.), *cert. denied* 534 U.S. 943 (2001).)

Pennsylvania has adopted a per se reversible error approach to biblical references in death penalty cases. In *Commonwealth v. Chambers*, 599 A.2d 630, 643 (Pa. 1991), *cert. denied*, 504 U.S. 946 (1992), the prosecutor argued, "Karl Chambers has taken a life. As the Bible says, 'and the murderer shall be put to death.'" The defense objected and the trial court immediately gave a curative instruction, but the Pennsylvania Supreme Court reversed, announcing a per se rule, stating: "We now admonish all prosecutors that reliance in any manner upon the Bible or any other religious writing in support of the imposition of a penalty of death is reversible error per se and may subject violators to disciplinary action." (*Id.* at 644.)

Courts usually find that Bible quotes and other religious imagery that do not ask the jury to follow religious teachings rather than the law are not per se reversible error. In those cases, courts typically take the approach endorsed by the Sixth Circuit that, although a prosecutor's statements that the Bible supported capital punishment were improper, the court could not "conclude that they so tainted the proceeding that they constitute reversible error. (*Coe v. Bell*, 161 F.3d 320, 351 (6th Cir. 1998).) The First Circuit similarly refused to reverse a conviction after a prosecutor compared a defendant's denial of intent to import cocaine with Peter's denial of Christ. The court found the religious reference to be an "irrelevant and [an] inflammatory appeal to jurors' private, religious beliefs," but held that "unambiguous evidence" and "strong and explicit" curative instructions prevented the religious references from constituting reversible error. (*United States v. Giry*, 818 F.2 120, 133–34 (1st Cir.), *cert. denied*, 484 U.S. 855 (1987).)

Most courts weigh the statements made in the context of the strength of the evidence of guilt and whether there has been a curative instruction to the jury. Reversals are rare when the religious references are few, the evidence of guilt is strong, and explicit curative instructions are given to the jury. Examples include *Hooks v. State*, 416 A.2d 189, 204–07 (Del. 1980), in which the court found that the prosecutor's statement that defendants were "'despicable' people to whom the Bible 'doesn't mean anything'" was improper but not prejudicial due to the weight of the evidence and curative instructions. In *State v. Cribbs*, 967 S.W.2d 773, 783–84 (Tenn. 1998), the court found that, although the prosecutor's references to the Bible were improper, the defendant was not prejudiced by invocation of the passage "whatever a person sows, so shall he reap" during the penalty phase of a capital trial because the prosecutor characterized it as a metaphor for individual responsibility.

Invited Response

Because of the prosecutor's inability to appeal in most instances, defense counsel's improper use of religion in closing argument remains largely unreviewed by appellate courts. But the de facto broader latitude defense lawyers enjoy due to lack of appellate control is counterbalanced by the invited response doctrine that allows prosecutors during rebuttal to respond in kind to defense improprieties. Although trial judges should enforce the limits of proper argument equally upon defense lawyers and prosecutors, when trial judges fail to do so, the ABA Standards for Criminal Justice provide that "a prosecutor may be justified in making a reply to an argument of defense counsel that may not have been proper if made without provocation." (Criminal Justice Standard 3-5.8 commentary.)

The Supreme Court in *United States v. Young*, 470 U.S. 1 (1985), approved the invited response doctrine when it reasoned that "defense counsel's conduct, as well as the nature of the prosecutor's response, is relevant" in deciding whether the prosecutor's remarks affected the fairness of the trial. (*Id.* at 12.) The Court affirmed the conviction while lamenting that "two improper arguments—two apparent wrongs—do not make for a right result." (*Id.* at 11.) The Court cautioned that its decisions on the invited response doctrine "should not be read as judicial approval—or encouragement—of response-in-kind that inevitably exacerbates the tensions inherent in the adversary process." (*Id.* at 12.) In explaining the doctrine, the Court stated that although the prosecutor's argument was improper, it did not mandate reversal because the prosecutor's remarks were "invited" and limited to respond to the defense remarks. (*Id.* at 12–13.)

Courts, then, will not reverse convictions when a prosecutor quotes from the Bible or uses other religious imagery in closing arguments if defense counsel did so first. For example, the court in *Bennett v. Angelone, supra*, 92 F.3d 1345–47, found the prosecutor's religious references to Noah's "sword of justice," Jesus, and the Romans were "highly improper and deserve strong condemnation" but not sufficient to render sentencing "fundamentally unfair" due to a curative instruction and the defense's use of religion in summation. And in *Crow v. State*, 458 S.E.2d 799, 811 (Ga. 1995), the Georgia Supreme Court found the prosecutor's statement that "the Bible says that you shall be put to death if you kill somebody" a reasonable response to defense evidence in mitigation based largely on "appeals to religion" including ministers and fellow churchgoers, "all of whom praised Crowe for his Christianity and religious activities, including past service as a minister of music and a deacon." The *Crowe* court found that the prosecutor "did not urge the jury to return a death sentence based on Crowe's religious beliefs or argue that the teachings of a particular religion command the imposition of the death penalty in the case," so even if the prosecutor's arguments were improper, they were a "legitimate effort" to counter the defense witnesses. (*Id.*)

Two Lessons

There are two clear lessons concerning the use of religious imagery and references in closing argument. First, the prosecutor should avoid religiously charged closing arguments in the first instance. Statements that assert that jurors have a religious duty to convict or impose specific penalties in a case are improper. The criminal justice system is a secular system, requiring jurors to reach their verdict by applying state or federal law to the evidence admitted during the trial.

Second, the defense lawyer also needs to be cautious about religious references. Although a defense lawyer does not run the risk of having a not guilty verdict overturned on appeal because the lawyer quoted from the Bible in closing arguments, by using religious references the defense may open the door to the prosecutor's use of religion in rebuttal argument. Should the prosecutor decide to interject religion into the rebuttal as an invited response, reversal based on the prosecutor's use of religion is un-likely, provided the prosecutor does not exceed the bounds of the defense's use of religion.

Conclusion

Studies show that most jurors make up their minds before closing arguments, and most trial lawyers agree that a case is won or lost during earlier phases of a trial. Yet lawyers continue to cross the ethical boundaries of proper argument by interjecting religion. Why do lawyers do it? Inexperience, lack of preparation, and ignorance of the limits of proper argument may explain the tendency. Passion for the case may also carry some lawyers away. Some may be unable to disengage their own religious convictions. Whatever the reasons, lawyers should keep religion out of their closing arguments so that jurors stay focused on applying the law. Criminal trials have serious consequences for the accused and the victims. When religion is interjected into closing arguments, a prosecutor faces the possibility of a reversal. Either the defense or the prosecution may trigger a mistrial. And the defense may invite a response-in-kind from the prosecutor, resulting in statements that would otherwise trigger a mistrial or be grounds for an appeal. The Ten Commandments do not belong in the courthouse rotunda, and religious references and imagery do not belong in closing arguments.

Resources for Chapter 23

Rules and Standards

Model Rule of Professional Conduct 3.4.
Criminal Justice Standards 3-5.8 and 4-7.7.

Cases and Ethics Opinions

People v. Simon, 252 P. 758 (Cal. App. 1927).
Berger v. United States, 295 U.S. 78 (1935).
Hooks v. State, 416 A.2d 189 (Del. 1980).
United States v. Young, 470 U.S. 1 (1985).
United States v. Giry, 818 F.2 120 (1st Cir.), *cert. denied*, 484 U.S. 855 (1987).
Commonwealth v. Chambers, 599 A.2d 630 (Pa. 1991), *cert. denied*, 504 U.S. 946 (1992).
Pennsylvania v. Daniels, 644 A.2d 1175 (Pa. 1994).
United States v. Levy-Cordero, 67 F.3d 1002 (1st Cir. 1995).
Crow v. State, 458 S.E.2d 799 (Ga. 1995).
Bennett v. Angelone, 92 F.3d 1336 (4th Cir.), *cert. denied*, 519 U.S. 1002 (1996).
DeFreitas v. State, 701 So. 2d 593 (Fla. Dist. Ct. App. 1997).
State v. Cribbs, 967 S.W.2d 773 (Tenn. 1998).
Coe v. Bell, 161 F.3d 320 (6th Cir. 1998).
Carruthers v. State, 528 S.E.2d 217 (Ga. 2000).
Sandoval v. Calderon, 241 F.3d 765 (9th Cir.), *cert. denied* 534 U.S. 943 (2001).
State v. Ceballos, 832 A.2d 14 (Conn. 2003).

Articles, Reports, Books, and Other Sources

Brian C. Duffy, *Barring Foul Blows: An Argument for a Per Se Reversible-Error Rule for Prosecutors' Use of Religious Arguments in the Sentencing Phase of Capital Cases*, 50 VAND. L. REV. 1335 (1997).
Monica K. Miller & Brian H. Bornstein, *Religious Appeals in Closing Arguments: Impermissible Input or Benign Banter*, 29 LAW & PSYCHOL. REV. 29 (2005).

TABLE OF CASES

INDEX